GHOSTS OF WALES

GHOSTS OF WALES

ACCOUNTS FROM THE VICTORIAN ARCHIVES

MARK REES

The History Press

All illustrations © Sandra Evans except where otherwise noted.

(www.facebook.com/SandraEvansArt)

First published 2017

The History Press
The Mill, Brimscombe Port
Stroud, Gloucestershire, GL5 2QG
www.thehistorypress.co.uk

© Mark Rees, 2017

British Library Cataloguing in Publication Data.
A catalogue record for this book is available from the British Library.

ISBN 978 0 7509 8418 8

Typesetting and origination by The History Press
Printed and bound by CPI Group (UK) Ltd, Croydon, CR0 4YY

CONTENTS

ABOUT THE AUTHOR

Mark Rees has worked in the media in Wales for more than fifteen years as the What's On editor and arts writer for the *South Wales Evening Post*, *Carmarthen Journal* and *Llanelli Star* newspapers, and *Swansea Life* and *Cowbridge Life* magazines.

During that time he has written and talked extensively on Halloween and paranormal subjects for the press, including conducting in-depth investigations into some of Wales' most haunted places.

His first book, *The Little Book of Welsh Culture*, was published by The History Press in 2016.

ACKNOWLEDGEMENTS

Writing a book is a team effort, and *Ghosts of Wales: Accounts from the Victorian Archives* would not have been possible without the very kind assistance of everyone who helped along the way, starting with Nicola Guy and the wonderful team at The History Press who commissioned my investigation into the Welsh ghosts of the nineteenth century.

A huge *diolch o'r galon* goes to the amazing Sandra Evans, whose superb illustrations have made this book worth owning for the art alone. To see more of Sandra's work, visit her Facebook page at: www.facebook.com/SandraEvansArt.

A collection of this nature would not have been possible without the invaluable service provided by those working hard in the newspaper archive industry, and my deepest thanks goes to everyone at The National Library of Wales in Aberystwyth and West Glamorgan Archive Service in Swansea.

I would also like to express my undying gratitude to my fantastic family for once again putting up with me during the writing and research of another book, and to everyone who has supported me on my publishing adventures to date, including: Jonathan Roberts and all at the *South Wales Evening Post*; Caroline Rees and all who made a success of *The Little Party of Welsh Culture*; Jane Simpson and all at Galerie Simpson; Kev Johns; Chris Carra; Owen Staton; Fifty One Productions; Rosie Davies; Mal Pope; Wyn Thomas; Pat Jones; the Heroes and Legends festival; Dan Turner and the

Horror 31 gang; Simon Davies and all at The Comix Shoppe; Ian Parsons; Ronnie Kerswell-O'Hara; Swansea Fringe Festival; and Emma Hardy and Bolly the cat, who ensured that I always had enough pizza and wine to keep me going, and that I was always awake nice and early enough to get on with my research – even on my days off.

INTRODUCTION

Do you believe in ghosts?

Tell anyone that you're writing a book called *Ghosts of Wales: Accounts from the Victorian Archives*, and that will be their number one question.

But it's a question which I think is almost irrelevant when it comes to writing, or reading, a book of this nature. Regardless of our own personal beliefs – hard-nosed sceptic, true believer, or undecided and sitting on the fence – what makes the accounts contained in this volume so fascinating, and possibly terrifying, is that for the people who experienced them, seeing – as well as hearing, feeling, and in some cases smelling – really was believing.

Not that everything in this book is considered to be fact, of course – even if it was reported as such at the time. Some of the accounts were proven to be false, others are incredibly hard to take seriously, and there are those with no evidence to back up the claims besides the words of an untrustworthy witness.

But then there are those which are much more difficult to disprove.

There are accounts which were corroborated by multiple, reliable sources. There are some which were argued about in the courts of law. There are others which eerily forewarned of upcoming events which came to pass. And many of them are verifiable with dates and addresses, recorded testimonies, and hard-to-know details included.

I think a more appropriate question to ask, and one which is much easier to answer, would be 'why the Victorian era?'

The Victorian era has been dubbed the 'golden age' for ghosts and spiritualism, in both fiction and the real world. During the nineteenth century, the likes of Charles Dickens and Edgar Allan Poe were sending shivers down readers' spines with their tales of unspeakable horrors, while the Fox sisters kick-started an Atlantic-crossing craze for séances in America, and the Society for Psychical Research was established to investigate claims in a scientific manner.

Much has been written on these subjects already, but while the misers of London were being shown the errors of their ways by Christmastime spirits, and the great and the good were sitting around tables listening for knocks from beyond the grave, what I really wanted to know more about were the spooky happenings in my home country – while the world was going paranormal crazy, where were all the Welsh ghosts?

There was only one way to find out. I decided to roll up my sleeves and do some good old-fashioned research in the newspaper archives. And I was totally unprepared for what I would find.

Initially, I had hoped to uncover a few good reports. But the more I dug, the more I found. They just kept coming, and seemed to get better and better all the time. Before I knew it, an hour or two's research to satisfy my curiosity become a day's research, and then a week's research, and then a month's research, and then a year's research.

What really excited me the most was that these were stories that I had never heard of before, and I was uncovering facts which might have gone unseen for more than a century. These weren't the same old yarns which have been repeated endlessly, but new tales, to me at least, of dark séances in Swansea, a noisy White Lady on the streets of Cardiff, and mysterious premonitions ahead of horrific mining disasters.

It was then that I decided that, to do these stories justice, it would be a good idea to collate my research into a book. Fortunately, my publisher agreed, and I'm pleased to say the copy that you now hold in your hands is the result of that pleasant discovery one Halloween.

Rather than simply throwing a series of unconnected stories together, I have presented them in such a way as to form, I hope, a coherent narrative which will take the reader on a journey through the many aspects of supernatural activity and beliefs at the time. Because while this book might be a collection of ghost stories, it also serves as a tantalising glimpse back at Welsh society in the Victorian era, when the dragons and fairies from days gone by gave way to much more frightening things which went bump in the night.

As such, it has been divided into nine sections, which range from the more traditional ghost stories firmly rooted in the folk tales of old, to the more sinister accounts of violent poltergeist attacks on secluded farmlands. Some of the reports provoked heated debates in the letters pages, and others warranted multiple follow-ups, and where possible I have collected all of the available information together into a single article. I have also corrected any spelling and grammatical errors which might have been included in the original newspaper reports, and tried to remain consistent with the spelling of place names where appropriate – for example, Aberystwyth has been spelt in the Welsh way throughout, except when used in the title of a publication such as *The Aberystwith Observer*.

How many of the accounts in this book are true? I will leave it up to you, dear reader, to approach them all with an open mind, and to decide for yourself.

I hope you enjoy reading this book as much as I enjoyed researching it, and if any of the locations are familiar to you, who knows – maybe you could pop along and see if the ghosts still haunt to this day?

Mark Rees, 2017

1

WILD WALES

Do you believe in ghosts? Then attend to my story! But first draw round a good fire, and get company to keep your courage up. Laugh as we may at the idea of ghosts and witchery, people do believe in ghosts, and fear them.

The Victorian era was a time of unprecedented change, for the people living through such turbulent times, as well as for the popularity of ghost stories – in the world of fiction as well as in the real world.

During Queen Victoria's reign, which ran from 1837 until her death in 1901, life was moving at a rapid pace. In Wales, the Industrial Revolution had seen communities transformed beyond recognition, with many leaving their traditional rural homes behind to find work in larger towns and cities. The country's population boomed, and an influx of immigration brought with it new influences and ideas.

The Victorian era was seen as an age of rationality, scientific progress and innovation – the ever-expanding railways enabled people to travel far and wide, the telegraph and telephone allowed for communication like never before, and Charles Darwin published the world-changing *On the Origin of Species* in 1859.

But it did not do away with paranormal beliefs. Far from it, in fact. Much like Darwin's theory they evolved and, if anything, became more popular than ever.

Charles Dickens' *A Christmas Carol*, considered to be one of the definitive ghost stories of the period, was published in 1843, and advances in the printed press saw a huge increase in demand for sensational spooky yarns to fill the periodicals. At the same time, stories which had previously been more of an oral tradition, such as the old Welsh folk tales of goblins and dragons, began to give way to modern explanations for unexplainable events – from now on, mysterious sounds heard at the dead of night were more likely to be attributed to the troubled spirit of a former occupant than a visit from the mischievous fairy folk, *y tylwyth teg*.

As we shall see in this book, interest in the paranormal was further bolstered by such factors as the rise of spiritualism, the conditions of living in crowded gas-lit homes, the new terrors which lurked deep underground in the mines, and more than a few practical jokers along the way, all of which played a part in keeping the supernatural firmly in the spotlight.

In this first chapter, we head out into the great outdoors to take a look at some of the strange occurrences which were reported in what are considered to be the more traditional haunted locations – the dark lonely forests, the dreamy romantic lakes, the grand old mansion houses, and the imposing mountains which combined to make up wild Wales.

The two-headed phantom

From Anne Boleyn to the Headless Horseman, spirits with severed heads have been a popular mainstay of ghost stories for centuries.

But in Abersychan in 1856, the opposite appeared to be true. The town's unique ghost, which was said to be 'haunting' the vicinity of the Blue Boar public house, wasn't missing his head – he had gained a second one.

The two-headed entity was described as having a 'hideous appearance', and had 'stricken many of the inhabitants with great terror, especially those whom he has honoured with a visit, or thought worthy of a glimpse of its outline', nearly driving one fearful local to an early deathbed.

In a newspaper report, multiple witnesses claimed that they could 'minutely describe him', and the believers in 'ghostly mysteries' put forward a theory as to his identity, as well as how he had managed to gain an extra head. As one resident explained:

> It is the ghost of an old man who suddenly met his death by falling down stairs and splitting his skull. The old man, when living, was an apostate from the Roman Catholic faith, therefore, could not have *rest* in the *other world*; consequently, he is a wanderer upon the face of this one. The cause assigned for his appearing with two heads is, that his head being split when dying, could not again be reunited; therefore, they are not really two heads, but two separate halves of the once whole.

The sceptical journalist, unconvinced by this hypothesis, asks, 'Is this the wisdom of the nineteenth century?!!', adding somewhat disbelievingly that those living in the immediate locality are too scared to leave their homes after dark unless 'some urgent necessity compels them'.

In the case of labourer Dan Harley, who is described as a 'true believer in apparitions', an urgent necessity did indeed compel him to stay out after dark one night and, as a result, he came face-to-face with the terrifying entity:

> Being delayed from returning home until a late hour, he had no alternative but to pass the haunted spot, or to have a night's parade in the chilly air. Not liking the latter, he determined to proceed despite his *dread*. He went on *courageously* until within a few yards of his lodging house, when he fancied

he could see something – he paused, and lo! it was no less than the dreaded *phantom*. He could not speak: neither could he move backward nor forward – he remained transfixed to the spot for several seconds, but as soon as he thought the spectre was disappearing, he made a desperate effort, and reached the house, wherein he repeated undefinable prayers to his preserver. His feelings for the remainder of the night can be imagined better than described. It is certain that he did not enjoy much rest, for he says that he was 'covered all over with fright'.

The next morning, Dan attempted to go to work as normal, but the event had proven to be too traumatic:

> On his way he sat down in a fainting state, the fright all over him still. At that time his fellow workman Patrick King happened to come by the place and, seeing his fellow comrade in such a weak state, assisted him home. For several days poor Harley was in a very desponding state. For some time he thought he was going to die, and under that conviction he wished his friends to give to his friend Pat Ring, after his death, the portrait of Ellen, his old sweetheart, which he held in great veneration; also his big pipe and his *backey pouch*.

Fortunately, he soon recovered – and kept hold of his possessions for a little while longer – but remained convinced of what he had seen that night:

> When he is spoken to now respecting his boasted courage, he says, very seriously, that he never was afraid, nor never will be afraid of all the ghosts of the earth or of the spirits of the air; but that such a two-headed monster was enough to put the dread on any man, and no man could help it, and 'Be jabers, I hope it may be the last I may ever see of the lad.'

A wild night by the romantic lakes

The following recollection of a ghostly encounter published in 1895 is an interesting story in and of itself, but what makes it potentially even more interesting is the name attributed to it: W.G. Shrubsole.

While the article does not give any further details as to the author's identity, the Victorian landscape painter William George Shrubsole was known to have been working in Wales during the period, having relocated to

Bangor in the 1870s, and his choice of words, as this introduction illustrates, would perfectly fit that of somebody in search of inspiration from the rugged landscape:

> I had been staying during the autumn of 188– at a cottage situated on the shores of one of the most romantic lakes in Wales. I grew so charmed with the place that I prolonged my stay until the beginning of December, and was amply rewarded by the wild beauty of effect which the scenery around ever presented.

Little did he realise that, by extending his stay, he would see not only more of the country's wild beauty, but also something of a much more otherworldly nature. The following events, as recalled by the writer himself, took place towards the end of his visit:

> On a moonlight night, I became the observer of what to me at the time seemed a strange, but by no means supernatural, manifestation. It was only by the light of what I afterwards heard that my experience assumed the complexion of the supernatural, and as at the time I was unexcited in mind, and not in expectation of any manifestation from another world, I am plunged in difficulties whenever I attempt to account for it by natural causes. Had my mind been in a state of highly wrought tension, I could easily account for the vision, by relegating it to that class of sensory illusions to which we well know mankind is susceptible, and of which I myself have had, on more than one occasion, very striking examples.
>
> Well, then, one evening after supper, at the close of a very uneventful day, I took a walk as far as the end of the lake and back. This was a very ordinary thing for me to do, and on the occasion in question, I lit my pipe, and with a stout stick in my hand, wended my way along the side of the lake, my only companion being a large dog belonging to the house. It was blowing up for a wild night, and now and again a gust swept down from the hollows of the hills with a violence that made me pause in my walk to steady myself and caused the surface of the lake to be whipped into temporary commotion; the moon shone fitfully through the driving clouds and ever and again there came a soughing from the towering crags around, strangely wild and human, as if the spirit of the wind were mourning amongst them.
>
> At last I reached the end of the lake, and giving a long look behind the dark dreary moorland, turned to retrace my steps towards the cottage. For some

time I made rapid progress homeward, noting the wonderful way in which the patches of moonlight chased each other up the side of a steep mountain on the opposite side of the lake, until I was nearly half way back to the cottage. At this spot the road formerly went round a point of land jutting into the lake, covered with huge masses of rock piled high one above another. When I reached this place the moon became densely overcast with clouds, and it suddenly grew so dark that I could scarcely see the wall on each side of the road.

The dog was some few yards in advance, and I called him, intending to stop for a minute in order to fill and light my pipe, hoping, too, that the clouds would soon break again. But the dog, instead of returning to my call, gave a short howl, which, a few moments later, I heard him repeat at a greater distance. He was evidently making for home as fast as possible, and I concluded that he must have trodden on something and hurt or cut his foot. Leaning against the wall, I struck a match and shielding it with my body and hands from the wind, succeeded in lighting my pipe, and then again the moon began to break through the clouds, and I paused for a few seconds to watch the light stealing across the water.

Suddenly below me at a few yards distance I saw the figure of an old man, his hair flying in the wind as he stooped forward to lean upon the handle of a spade or mattock. I was startled, for the old fellow came so suddenly into view that it seemed as if he must have dropped there from the clouds. I hailed him with a shout of 'A wild night this' – he gave no reply, but slowly turned his face up towards mine. The moon gleamed out brightly for an instant, and I saw a pair of hollow, sunken eyes set in a face so full of a kind of weary despair – of a hungry disappointment – that I was shocked, and for a moment I had a slight feeling that there was something 'uncanny' in the appearance of this old man at such a time. What *could* he be doing there? But I had no time to lose; it was getting late, so with a 'Good night' shouted in the local vernacular I turned towards home once more. A few paces further on I looked back, but the old fellow was gone – had probably moved into the shadow of, or behind some of the rocks.

Putting my best foot foremost, I soon reached the cottage and found the kitchen tenanted by three or four people from neighbouring farms. 'Dear me! Mr —,' said the good woman, 'We have been quite anxious about you, sir, since Tos came in without you. Something seemed to have frightened him.'

'Oh! I am all right,' I replied with a laugh. 'By-the-bye, can you tell me who the old fellow is I saw along the shore of the lake with a spade?'

I shall not forget the effect of my simple query. Every eye turned on me with a ghastly stare, the men turned pale, and the woman sank into a chair. One of the men turned to another and in accents that seemed dry and forced said: 'He has seen the digger of Fotty.'

Then their tongues were loosened and a Babel of Welsh arose. In vain I tried to understand what they were saying. I could only catch a word here and there. But they soon departed after many pitying glances at me and much ominous shaking of heads.

Then I learnt the cause of this commotion – I had seen a ghost! The figure of the old man was that of one who had died several years back. During his lifetime he had been remarkable for the penury of his habits, and was said to have on more than one occasion taken the most relentless advantage of people in monetary difficulties; his greedy and miserly habits became a monomania, and this, at last, assumed the form of a hallucination that there was a vast treasure buried at 'Fotty' – the place where I saw him. At all hours the old miser might be seen there digging in different places in spite of wind and weather, and he would often be heard muttering colloquies with someone he seemed to imagine was at his elbow, so it soon got reported that he was in league with the fiend, and he was avoided and detested by the neighbours more than ever in consequence.

At last, one stormy day, a fisherman found the old man's dead body at 'Fotty' with his spade still grasped in his hand. The discoverer ran in alarm to the nearest farm-house to inform the people of the miser's death, and a party of men soon made their way to the spot where the fisherman had left the body; but it was gone, spade and all, and never a trace of it was seen again. Sometime after, what was stated to be the handle of the old man's spade was found in an almost inaccessible hollow of the neighbouring mountains, so it became accepted as Gospel truth that the fiend had carried away the miser's body over the mountains and dropped the spade in the transit. After this a farmer returning home late one night was frightened almost to death by seeing what he took to be the spirit or the miser, spade in hand, at work on his favourite spot. The story got abroad, again and again it was verified, the ghost of the old miser from time to time appeared to several, and seemed to be, as a role, the portent of the direst calamity to each individual who saw it.

This was the story as I received it, and its truth was corroborated by many people living in the locality. Had it been told me *before* I saw the figure by the lake, I should have simply thought the apparition the figment of my imagination; but at the time I saw the old man, I knew nothing of him or his history, so I cannot account for the vision by any process of reasoning, and I am driven to the conclusion that as Shakespeare says: 'There are more things in heaven and earth, Horatio, than are dreamt of in our philosophy.'

The haunted hiding place

Plas Mawr, Conwy by Arthur Baker (1888).

A room in Plas Mawr, 'one of the most perfectly preserved specimens of Elizabethan manor houses now existing in this country', made the headlines in 1893 following the report of a haunted room.

The recently formed Royal Cambrian Academy of Art, an institution for the visual arts in Wales, had based itself at the property in Conwy which contained 'numerous low, oak-panelled, and oak-floored rooms, filled with an excellent collection of oil and water colours, of which the critics speak very highly'.

It drew many visitors to see the art and architecture, but after the publication of the following account, people were soon visiting to see another of its attractions – a ghost.

A member of the public got straight to the point when he brought the haunting to light in a letter to the press:

I wish to make public – for the first time, I believe – an attraction that one almost instinctively looks for in connection with such an old house as Plas

Mawr, and that is 'A Haunted Room!' There can be no doubt about it, for I have the story from one who is both an eye and an ear-witness of the fact that one of the rooms in Plas Mawr is haunted.

He explained that the story had been related to him by one of the Royal Cambrian Academy of Art's officials who, on finding the narrator and his companion exploring a particular part of the house, introduced himself with the enticing opening line, 'Ah, you are studying the haunted room, are you?'

At first they laughed, but the official continued, relating his first-hand experiences at the premises:

'Very few people know it,' he said, 'but it is a fact, and it is supposed to have some connection with the priest's hiding place, which is just here,' he added, tapping the wall between the door of the room and the huge fireplace.

We were delighted, and explained that we had not heard of the priest's hiding place any more than we had of the haunted room, and begged of him to let us see the interesting secret recess in which, perhaps, some poor recusant had hidden himself in the stern times of Good Queen Bess.

'Come this way,' he said, and advancing to the corner of the room, he tapped the apparently solid wall. We expected to see the wall open, revealing a dark cavity, but nothing happened, and somewhat disappointed, we listened to our guide's explanation that 'the hiding place lay behind the wall.'

He led the pair through two rooms and up a flight of stairs where a 'small worm-eaten door' led to a low attic. They were warned to follow in the guide's footsteps exactly, 'otherwise you may crash through the ceiling of the room below,' and he directed them towards the attic's top right-hand corner:

There we saw a recess about five feet in depth, and about four feet wide. It is uncovered now, and would afford no security against the most superficial search; but in the old days it was cunningly and heavily covered so that even tapping the covering would not betray the cavity beneath. But this was not the whole of the hiding place. If by chance the pursuers discovered this recess, and managed to open the trap door, no fugitive would be visible, for the inner side of the hiding place consisted of a sliding panel, which gave entrance into an 'inner sanctuary' into which the fugitive would slip, on finding that his first hiding place had been discovered, leaving nothing for the pursuer to gaze at but an empty space. Of course the chances were a hundred to one against the pursuers suspecting the existence of an anteroom, and so the hunted priest would, let us hope, escape.

This was Plas Mawr's 'priest hole', around which the ghostly activity was said to take place:

He says that he was alone in the building late one night, writing. He had been round every room before that, previous to closing, to see that all the visitors had left the house for that day. Suddenly, in the silence of the night, he heard a measured footfall begin to pace the room over his head. He listened for a long time. The measured footfall continued, till he, not liking to go up alone, and in the dark, left, and went home.

Another time, he and his wife happened to be walking together in the courtyard below, when they both chanced to look up at the open window of the haunted room. He saw something withdrawing quickly from the window as he looked up. He said nothing to his wife for fear of alarming her, but at supper she remarked to him that when she chanced to look up at the window she thought she saw something or somebody withdraw quickly from the window. He also assures me that on several occasions when he has been in that room at dusk (he is not at all afraid of ghosts), he has heard or felt something pattering round him. Not merely round his feet; as a dog, cat, or rat might do, but brushing lightly against his body, at the same time making audible footsteps on the oaken floor. He concluded by saying that though he had not the slightest belief in ghosts, he can never enter that room even in broad daylight without a queer feeling coming over him, a kind of cold shivering.

At the end of his narrative, the author was keen to stress that the haunted room should in no way deter people from paying the mansion house a visit, and that it should be seen as an 'additional attraction … in this very charming old house, one of the sights of Conwy'.

Following the article's publication, stories of ghost sightings at Plas Mawr continued in other periodicals throughout the Victorian period, and in a follow-up in 1897 it was said that the ghost could be seen on a particular day of the year, 27 September, when it is believed to 'become visible'.

The murdered knight

In 1897, the following 'creepy' story was told to a reporter by 'an intelligent official of a Glamorganshire school board'.

It was while walking the Breconshire countryside for the benefit of his 'health and change' that he decided to visit a relation who was working in a nearby secluded farmhouse. Described as somebody who was not pre-disposed to believing in the paranormal beforehand – he was a 'shrewd, common sense man whose chief hobby is Welsh etymology' – by the end of his stay, he was convinced enough to investigate the paranormal further. What follows is his account, as narrated to the correspondent:

While on a tramp, about half-way between Brecon and Builth, he came to an old-fashioned farm, possessing some manorial characteristics: dormer win-dows, gables, with a large walled garden and an amplitude of ivy. It was a house which had seen better days. At present a farmer and his wife and one maid-servant occupied it, living a quiet, uneventful life. The official knew that a relative of his was servant there, and hence his call at the old place, and, from being invited to tea, he was asked to sleep there. He accepted this readily, as it was a long walk to even a roadside inn.

He went to bed, and in the middle of the night woke up as sharply as if it had been daybreak, with an uncomfortable feeling of chilliness and an impression that there was someone in the room. He remained perfectly quiet, and in a second or two was aware of a faint luminous appearance, and saw a filmy outline of a figure in armour. He could see no head, but the armour was very distinct. He spoke in a quiet, soothing voice, saying, 'Whoever you are, make yourself visible to me, and speak; I am not afraid,' and a slightly increased force of vision resulted, as if the form was endeavouring to fulfil his wish, but gradually the luminosity disappeared, and he fell asleep.

In the morning his relative the maid-servant, an unsophisticated girl as innocent as the day, asked him, cheerily, how he slept, and the official, trying to find out if his experience was unique or not, gave an evasive reply, saying, 'A capital bed, girl; very comfortable indeed.' 'And you were not disturbed, uncle?' she continued. 'In what way do you mean?' 'Well,' she said, 'they do say the room is haunted, and one or two who have slept there have seen a figure, wearing tin things on, or something like dish covers.'

This satisfied the inquirer that someone else had witnessed the vision, and that it was no fancy of his own. He purposes another quiet visit and further investigation. 'I am not afraid,' he added, in conclusion. 'It cannot hurt me, and I am satisfied that there is something in it. The tradition in the locality is that a knight was murdered by another.'

A phantom coach with a headless driver

In 1895, a correspondent from the parish of Whitford in Flintshire lamented the decline of traditional spooky stories in the area, and redressed the balance somewhat by recalling three of their own.

In the first story, a workman and his wife moved into a vacant cottage in the high parts of the village, but after a single night fled back to their original dwelling:

The man with his amiable spouse were seen one autumn day busily engaged removing their household goods and lowly livestock into their new tenancy. When the shades of evening had covered the sky, the worthy husband was allowed by his generous wife to visit the nearest alehouse to partake of a well-earned glass of beer. In a short time there burst into the public house a woman breathless and trembling and said to her husband 'Tyd adref, Tom, mae'r c— hefa'r geir' (she called him home in Welsh). Up jumped Tom and started for his new home manfully and courageously threatening vengeance on one and all who dare play jokes on his poor but amiable spouse who was hesitatingly following him. The night was calm and cloudless. In the distance lights could be seen in many a cottage showing that the wearied occupants had not as yet retired to their rest. The couple warily entered the house where all appeared still and peaceful. The owner drew his chair to the fire, the wife moved the round table close to her husband, and placed a lighted candle thereon. The master was calmly smoking the pipe of peace, and the mistress was sitting and nervously twirling her thumbs, and staring at the dying embers in the fireplace, when suddenly there was heard an awful din and a horrible noise, which caused the courage of Tom to ooze through his finger ends. Up he jumped, down went the table, out went the light; straight to the door he steered, hatless and bootless, and hurried away across the fields, and neither stopped nor stayed till he landed in his old home, and joined by his wife passed the night in misery surrounded by the empty walls. The next day processions consisting of man and wife carrying their belongings to their old habitation were seen, and happy they remain to this day, and the other house was left to the undisturbed possession of Mr Ghost.

In the second story, 'some holy ladies' in search of larger premises near the parish rented a house, but were 'disturbed nightly by mysterious noises and scratchings'. A nobleman and a friend with an interest in ghosts offered to investigate, but found nothing of note and were 'doomed to disappointment'.

But it is the third and final story which is the most notable of the trio, featuring a haunted coach with a headless driver:

One dark but starry night last October, a pious deacon of a neighbouring chapel was on a journey from his respectable home between the hours of one and two in the morning, and in all probability seriously engaged in spiritual devotions, and quietly contemplating the starry firmament, when suddenly and noiselessly he beheld a carriage full of quiet godly men, drawn by a couple of spirited steeds guided by a headless Jehu, coming from the direction of a noble mansion and going on the way to a religious establishment. When the story got noised abroad among the inhabitants near the way the carriage travelled, neither woman nor child could be seen out of doors after dusk even to do any household work, and people travelling will give this road and mansion the widest berth. Unfortunate beings feel a creeping sensation if they must traverse any part of that road.

2

HAUNTED HOMES

There is a tremor in female breasts, manly knees make friendly calls against each other, and the children's voices are hushed beneath the bedclothes.

Today, we might think of the home as one of the most natural places in the world for a ghost to while away their afterlife. From the printed page to the silver screen, we have been inundated with all manner of tales in which paranormal activity is focused solely on the family household.

But until the Victorian era this was still a novel idea, and spirits were more likely to be associated with ancient locations of a more suitably Gothic nature, dwelling in crumbling castles and lonely woodlands.

One reporter, who was sent to investigate strange behaviour in a newly built residential property in Wales, observed that:

> of old time the haunts of spirits were old castles and manor-houses grey with age and remote from men and cities, the phantoms that frequented them always appeared well armed with horrible excuses for their untimely reap-pearance. It would appear, however, that your modern spectre is 'of earthlier make,' for to the scene of this story I must take you not to the moated grange, or the ivy-covered manor house, but to a newly-built street.

Another correspondent noted that having a ghost in your house could actually increase, not decrease, the value of the property. If the owners could 'assure intending purchasers that a real ghost made some parlour, cellar or attic his own wherein he could exercise his nightly pranks during the long winter nights', buyers would surely be much more interested.

But after centuries of confining themselves to the shadowy outskirts of society, why were they suddenly disturbing people in their sole place of refuge?

Ghosts were undoubtedly in vogue and very much on Victorian people's minds at the time, from the popular works of supernatural fiction to an evening's entertainment at a séance. At the same time, families were living through an unprecedented period of anxious upheaval, with the search for work forcing them to live further apart than ever before. After relocating to modern houses with their modern sounds, dwelling in often cramped conditions and surrounded by unfamiliar faces in a brave new world, it's hardly surprising if the imagination ran wild occasionally as they watched their old way of life evaporating before their very eyes.

One theory for the growth in reports of ghosts in the home during this period is, quite simply, the lighting. For those sat at home, reading and talking about such ethereal matters by candle and gas light, the flickering – or, even worse, the unexpected extinguishing – of a light alone could cause a fright. On top of that, there are some who think that the carbon monoxide released from the gas lamps could also have induced hallucinations.

Or maybe the houses had actually been haunted all along, and it wasn't until the press began to report on such activity that the occupiers' supernatural cohabitants were brought to light ...

Wraith of a murderer stalks abroad

In July 1898, 'a terrible murder was committed' in Powell Street, Swansea, the details of which were reported in the local press:

> Henry O'Neill, alias Price, a seaman whose steps had been dogged by persistent misfortune, slaughtered his young wife in a most brutal fashion. Whilst in bed together he suddenly became frenzied, and inflicted innumerable stabs upon her, almost any one of which would have been sufficient to cause death. Subsequently O'Neill plunged into the canal close by, and put an end to his own existence.

It was a gruesome crime, but the story did not end there.

The murderer's house was soon re-occupied, and twelve months after he he had taken his own life, the ghost of the killer was said to be back at his old residence, scaring his former neighbours who were 'much perturbed by strange happenings'. It was claimed that:

> several of the residents affirm they have seen O'Neill's ghost. His spirit walks at night in the garden of number forty-five. The result is that the folk living on that side of Powell Street are in a terrible state of fright. As soon as the shades of night fall the back doors are locked, bolted and barred, and the women and children will not go out into the yards.

The sightings vary, but what follows are some of the descriptions of the encounters:

> One woman says she was reading downstairs late at night, when she saw O'Neill peering in at her through the window. She quickly joined her husband between the sheets. Another woman says she was taking in some clothes after dark, when two clammy hands were laid on her face, and she

was just in time to see O'Neill's spirit vanish into thin air. The people who have seen him walking restlessly about the garden of number 45 are many. He always seems to make for the corner where the murdered woman's clothes were buried. Mrs Williams, who lives at number 45, was at first sceptical. She laughed at the fears of her neighbours. Now she does not know what to make of it. A few days ago she dug up her garden so as to have a soft surface. Sure enough next morning footsteps were visible leading to the fateful spot in the corner.

A watch was set up, with three men keeping an eye out all night on one occasion, but they 'failed to lay the ghost by the heels'. As a result, the people of Powell Street were said to be in a 'terrible state of fright', and 'one little boy who saw the apparition has been rendered seriously ill'.

The publication's advice to any locals who might be fearful of the ghost? 'The people living in the street should bring a little common-sense to bear on the subject.'

Lively doings at Burry Port

A report of a musical ghost in Burry Port caused 'quite a noise' in 1899, with the initial story provoking a heated debate in the Carmarthenshire community.

It all began when a Mr and Mrs Phillips rented a property and claimed to witness all manner of strange phenomena. The accounts were brought to the attention of a 'cute penciller' from the Llanelli press who, along with a sergeant of police, went along to investigate.

On arrival, they found Mrs Phillips 'engaged with the wash tub', and after waking her husband Mr Owen Phillips, who had been working the night shift at the nearby copperworks, they recalled the events:

On the Thursday night, her husband and herself retired about half-past ten, leaving their two sons, William, aged twenty, and Owen, eighteen, downstairs. Shortly afterwards, when going to their room, they bade their parents 'Good-night,' and for a time all seems to have been oblivion. Then, Mrs Phillips went on: 'About half-past one on Friday morning I heard a chair moving, and then I heard the piano playing a tune, very slowly, and I says to myself, "Sure, there's somebody up very early!"'

At this point Mr Phillips, after remarking that he was roused by his wife, took up the thread from the latter. 'Aye,' said he, 'I says, "There's somebody playing a Jew's harp, to be sure."Then all at once it stopped and started again a little bit louder, and I was afraid of the wife getting a feared. So I says to her, "What's the matter, missus? It's only one of the boys downstairs," and I told her I should have to put the piano key in my pocket o' nights, or else the neighbours would surely be complaining about it. She said, "Aye, it's the only way to stop it," and then something struck her, for she says, "Nay, but didn't the boys come to bed some time back and say Good-night to us?" I said, "Yes, I know that they did," and then she asked me, "Well, whatever is it that's there?" So I says "I'll go down and see."And with that I jumped out of bed, but the missus got hold of me by the shoulder and begged of me not to go.'

Ignoring his wife's wishes, Mr Phillips went to investigate, and what follows is a conversation recorded by the reporter of the couple describing the events:

Mrs Phillips: I called 'Lord, have mercy on our souls!' Oh, how it did frighten me! (The reporter notes that Mrs Phillips interjected with this observation several times, and 'for the sake of brevity we omit the repetitions'.)

Mr Phillips: I asked her to be quiet and say nothing until we heard it again, so we sat down on the side of the bed, both of us for fully five minutes. It started again, the piano, you know, and then I went to the boys' room and pushed the chair away.

Mrs Phillips: Yes, I'd told the boys to put a chair behind the door because we had heard the ghost the night before.

Mr Phillips: And after I got my arm in the bedroom and pushed the chair away, William says to me – he had heard it, sir, and lying flat on his back with his eyes open – 'Who's playing the piano, dad?' And I says back to him, 'Nay, that's what I want to know.' He was terribly frightened, too. However, we came downstairs together, and as we were coming down the stairs the piano-playing stopped of a sudden. My! wasn't it beautiful. We looked all over the kitchen, in the back place, in the cupboards, under all the chairs and tables, and everything was in its place. The parlour door was found open, but it was locked on Thursday night. The cover of the piano was thrown back.

Mrs Phillips: And this chair was left just like this. I heard it being dragged from that corner over there, and that's what awakened me, because I'm not a very sound sleeper.

Mr Phillips: We must have disturbed him, for he finished the tune sudden-like. And wasn't it a lovely tune!

Mrs Phillips: It wasn't like anybody practising. It was lovely, everything was finished and perfect. We were listening to it for fully ten minutes, sat on the side of the bed. It wasn't any of (Ira D.) Sankey's tunes, for my husband knows all of them. The ghost is a heavy footed one; it's not a woman, it must be a man. We could hear it the night before walking about the landing, and it went in the boys' room. That's why I told them to put a chair behind the door. I thought at first it was Owen, because he was not very well, but he was fast asleep, and he didn't answer me. The ghost opened the little window at the top of the stairs, and jumped down on to the landing, making a big noise, and afterwards walking about quite bold-like. Now all the doors were bolted, except the one in the kitchen which I had left open, and I was terribly upset. Lor, I was nearly gone, because I have but poor health. I shall be bound to move from here, else I shall surely be dead. Lor! wasn't Owen, my husband, afraid. He was as white as this tablecloth.

Mr Phillips: I thought at first it was a man, but it struck me afterwards that if a fellow wanted to rob the place he would do it quietly, and not play the piano to awaken everybody. The first time I heard it it ran through me, and I was shaking like a leaf.

And so ended their account of that particular incident. But that wasn't the only ghostly activity to have occurred at the property, and Mr Phillips recalled a time when he was 'carrying a lamp, and it was blown out', adding that 'the house is alive'.

His wife also had a few more tales of her own:

I had a daughter, and she was going to be married. She put a big picture in the corner of the kitchen, leaning straight against the wall. I have another daughter, a young one, and in the morning she heard somebody walking about the house. So she awakens me and says, 'Mother, there's somebody in the house. I can hear them,' and with that – my husband was working night shift – we both comes downstairs. And do you think the picture was as we'd left it? No, the chair there had been pulled away and the picture shifted. We looked all over and couldn't find anything, so we went back to bed.

Another time my daughter, who was married, heard something. She has a pretty good nerve – she's 27 – so she awakened me and went down stairs. As she got to the bottom, which leads into the passage, there was a report like a gun going off, and she screams and runs upstairs, and when she gets to the top she looks round and she could see him in the passage all like white foam. She was sure it was a man; it wasn't a woman. My! wasn't she upset! She screamed murder, and would not go to her husband, but comes in my room and shouts, 'Oh, mother, mother, it's here, but I can't see it.' If my daughter was here now she'd tell you the same tale, and I'm sure she's glad she's living in Swansea now and not here.

Now, just to show you how bold that ghost is, about four months back I had a nephew of mine down from Swansea, and he slept in one of the front rooms next to mine. His bed was under the window, and he shouted out, 'Oh, auntie, auntie, somebody's thrown me against the wall.' My daughter and her husband were in another room, and the noise brought them out of their sleep. We could hear the ghost walking about, and the footsteps were plainly heard. It was in the middle of night, and my daughter lit the candle and was walking slowly from the room to the little boy's room when the candle was blown clean out. We could hear the 'puff.' Sure and it's true, quite true. After that I lit the candle again, and we all came downstairs.

Mrs Phillips admitted that some people might find their experiences hard to believe – the reporter himself had chuckled during the interview. But as if to preempt any backlash after the article's publication, she related a recent conversation with one such 'sceptical young man', and the daughter of a previous tenant, Mary Jane. Mrs Phillips claimed that Mary Jane's mother, Mrs Thomas, who now lived in Spring Gardens, had 'left the house two years ago because it was haunted':

I called to the girl and asked, 'Mary Jane, where did you have this ghost moving about?' and she said, 'I'll tell you, for the most part it was from the front room to the other one, over the landing,' and that is just where he goes now. I wish to goodness he would show himself and let us finish with him.

The article was published, and a week later the landlord of the property, David John Badger from Gladstone Terrace in Aberbeeg, felt obliged to respond to the allegations, and brought to light a possible ulterior motive that the couple might have for seeing a ghost on his premises:

Dear Sir, – My attention has been drawn to an article in your last issue entitled 'The Haunted House at Burry Port.' I regret that you have seen fit to publish such trivial nonsense, and to pander to the extreme credulity of several highly imaginative individuals. I must, however, ask you to deal with the matter in your next issue in such a manner as to utterly destroy the odium that would necessarily attach itself to the house by the publication of your article. I think you will have no objection to complying with my request since you must acknowledge it but fair. Common justice necessitates such a course of action since I need hardly point out that if the tale is believed the house is ruined. I may add that Mr Phillips has received notice to quit, and will be compelled to leave the premises as soon as possible. That will probably 'lay' the ghost.

The landlord wasn't the only correspondent unhappy with the article, and the 'sceptical young man' whom Mrs Phillips had used as evidence went even further in attempting to debunk the story. He was identified as being named 'Shellan, and he keeps a weigh-house in Caraway Street. Formerly he was a soldier. The hand-writing throughout, including the supposed signatures, is the same':

Dear Sir, – In reply to your statement re the Ghost of Burry Port, we the 'Persons' referred to, do hereby send in the following account, of the conversation with Mrs Phillips. I, the person referred to as the sceptical young man, was talking with Mrs Phillips telling her it was only fancy, as I did not believe in ghosts at all, when the daughter of Mrs Thomas of Spring Gardens, was passing at the time. Mrs Phillips said, 'Mary Jane you are just the person I was wishing to see. Didn't you leave this house because you heard noises in the house?' Mary Jane replied, 'I never heard anything at all while we were living in the house, the reason we left the house was because it is so open at the back. As for ghosts we never heard or saw anything of them.' In witness hereof we send this account, which is true and accurate in every detail. (Signed) Mrs Thomas, Mary Jane, and a Sceptical Young Man.

But the letters weren't all negative. One reader who defended the family, C. Ware from Exeter, offered a 'spiritualistic view' of events, including advice on how they could conduct a séance of their own to communicate with the ghost:

Sir, – I have read with much interest the particulars relating to the haunted house at Burry Port. If the occupants of the disturbed dwelling could become acquainted with the methods familiar to modern spiritualists for communicating with unseen intelligences of that kind it would be a great advantage to them, and probably much light would thereby be thrown upon the strange proceedings. If a few persons were to seat themselves around a small table (the number does not signify so long as they can sit comfortably), laying their hands lightly thereon, those unseen operators would readily respond to their overtures. Let them ask questions: three taps will be given for 'Yes,' and one tap for 'No.' Let them persevere with this experiment, singing a hymn whilst they sit. I, sir, have been familiar with all the wonderful phenomena of modern Spiritualism for about twenty years, and should any person connected with the haunted house, or, indeed, any of your readers, be disposed to communicate with me I will be happy to help them with any suggestions or information that I can give. In any house or in any company these unseen friends will respond to our overtures provided we are willing to observe the simple conditions whereby they can do so.

With so much public interest generated by the reports, and with both sides holding their ground, the newsman naturally decided to return to the scene for a follow-up story. When the allegations from the landlord were put to Mr and Mrs Phillips, they confirmed that they had been asked to vacate the premises, with the threat that if they weren't gone by the following Monday their rent would be doubled.

But they remained adamant that they were telling the truth, and Mrs Phillips 'refused to withdraw a single word she had uttered', saying that she hoped the next tenant to take the property would encounter the ghost on their first night in the premises.

She added that 'seeing is believing,' and to be able to see a ghost 'is reserved for those born in the early morning to associate with spirits. She was born early one morning, and not only has she seen ghosts, but had touched one!'

At this point, to further illustrate her claim that she was 'associated with spirits', Mrs Phillips recalled some previous encounters which had happened while living in Swansea about two years previously:

One night her married daughter, then single, was out later than usual, and Mrs Phillips and a female friend started off to go to the house where she was staying. On the way they passed Ebenezer Chapel, and Mrs Phillips seeing what she took to be her daughter, exclaimed, 'Hallo, my child, you're coming home.' At the same time she touched the supposed daughter on the shoulder, over which was thrown a grey cape, and then in an instant the head disappeared exactly like a Jack in the Box, and the apparition went through the

Ebenezer Baptist Church in Swansea, where an apparition is said
to have gone through the keyhole. (Ham)

keyhole of the chapel door. That very same ghost had previously found fun
in chasing a young lady who was cleaning out the chapel several times round
the graveyard; and Mrs Phillips fancied it was the disturbed occupier of a
grave that had just been opened!

On another occasion the ghost knocked loudly at Mrs Phillips' kitchen window, and when she and her little girl came downstairs and looked out, it, or rather she, called out in a mournful and solicitous tone, 'Go to bed, go to bed.' To which Mrs Phillips replied, 'I'll give you go to bed if I come out, I tell you.' Apparently this angered the ghost for she opened wide her mouth so that the teeth were prominent like miniature tusks, the eyes were fiery, and the view altogether was hideous. 'And you should have seen us run upstairs,' said Mrs Phillips.

Yet for all of Mrs Phillips' remonstrating, the Burry Port ghost failed to make a return appearance, and in conclusion the reporter offered their own suggestion on the no-show with reference to the area's latest supernatural hotspot:

His absence from the house is partly explainable. Spring cleaning is proceeding just now, and being fastidiously inclined, his present temporary haunt is the Copper Works Tip, from where he can get the ozone fresh and pure. Several persons speak to having seen him there last Thursday and Friday evenings.

Whisked away by a hideous apparition

Just before Halloween in 1893, a fantastical tale emerged from the Rhondda where a woman claimed that she was – quite literally – swept off her feet and whisked away by a spirit.

The whole village of Llwynypia was said to be gossiping about the event, and while the claims might seem a little far-fetched when compared to some of the other accounts in this book, it did result in a heated debate in the newspaper's letter pages.

The reporter begins with an overview of events, outlining the commotion caused by the visitation:

Great excitement has prevailed during the past few days at Llwynypia and the adjacent districts in consequence of startling allegations made by Mr John Dunn and his wife, who reside at 8, Amelia Terrace, Llwynypia, and also by several neighbours. These persons state that for several nights past hideous apparitions have been witnessed, and unaccountable peculiar noises heard, in the bedrooms and other parts of the cottage.

The premises have been visited by hundreds of persons during the past two or three days, and watched by Sergeant Hoyle, PC Pearce, and the other constables for hours in the evening, but nothing unusual has been discovered by them. On Thursday evening a well-known quoiter and a number of footballers stood for some time in front of the cottage, eagerly waiting the appearance of the ghost, and it is stated that the bravest of the football men was suddenly startled by an alleged supernatural visitant.

The journalist, accompanied by local schoolmaster Mr Tom John, the Welsh representative on the executive committee of the National Union of Teachers, then paid a visit to Mrs Dunn's cottage to try and establish the facts:

The house is a four-roomed one with a pantry adjoining one of the rooms near the back door. As we paced along the terrace, consisting of about twenty houses, situated on the mountainside, men and women were standing on the thresholds discussing the matter. We entered the cottage and found Mrs Dunn standing by a tub upon a chair washing some wearing apparel. 'Is this the house where the ghost has been causing disturbance?' I asked. 'Yes, sir; take a chair, gentlemen, if you please.' We seated ourselves immediately at her request, and then she unfolded her strange story.

'On Wednesday evening, about nine o'clock, I was standing near the pantry door, and suddenly the back door opened, and a tall apparition robed in white appeared close by me right before my eyes. I shrieked, and instantly it stretched forth both arms and clutched me tightly. There was no one in the house besides myself at the time. I lost my senses, and found myself shortly afterwards in an outhouse. The ghost told me there that he was going to take me away with him. I was dumb, could not utter a word for some time. There he kept me, holding me upon the wooden seat, and telling me in Welsh to raise a brick for him. I could not do so. The scones and the few bricks moved, and a rattle was heard by me. Then I was lifted up bodily and taken out and raised up into the air, and I lost my senses again. Afterwards, when I came to myself I found myself by the brink of a pond lower down on the hill-side, and he threatened to chuck me into the water and drown me. In taking me there the ghost had to lift me over a fence seven feet high. This house has been troubled by the ghost for nearly seven months off and on, but it is during the past few days that we have been greatly disturbed. Men living in this locality have been sleeping in turns upstairs for days past for the purpose of getting to the bottom of the matter. They hear the latch rattling and rapping on the doors and noises like the shuffling of feet and the clatter of crockery, and they can't see anything.'

Mrs Dunn said that the ghost spoke to her in a mixture of English and Welsh, quoting the ghost as saying 'Mae rhaid i ti ddyfod gyda mi' ('You have to come with me'), while she spoke only in Welsh in return. Also, on the night proceeding the reporter's visit, she had also received 'his ghostly assurance' that she 'would have peace in future, and that he would not torment her again'.

Mrs Dunn's husband, Jack from Somersetshire, had also been 'troubled by the spectre, and he sincerely believed it was a ghost'. He said that the 'pond has been visited by hundreds of people during the past day or two, and they all marvel at the strength of the "goblin" in lifting or conveying the landlady over the high fence'.

Some of the neighbours joined them in the kitchen and 'enlivened the proceedings' by recalling what they had seen and heard themselves. One of them described the assailant as wearing 'a pair of moleskin trousers, I think, and a white sheet over his shoulders'. When the reporter asked the obvious question – 'It was not a man, was it?' – he provided further details: 'No, because he vanished into air all at once, and then appeared before our very eyes and went off again.'

Another neighbour described seeing the 'shadow of the ghost on the wall opposite her house, and she thought the ghost was wearing corduroy breeches'. She added that a 'Christian young man, and very religious, was one of the men who were sitting up in turns all night in the house, and he had experienced the very same thing as they and Mrs Dunn had'.

One of the group also offered a possible identity for the entity:

An old man was taken to the asylum from here many years ago, and he wore ribbed trousers and moleskin trousers sometimes, and I think his spirit has returned to look for a bag of gold which, it is said, he left behind. A lot of people have been searching the place for money yesterday.

But while the Dunns and their neighbours were clearly convinced of the ghost's authenticity, the police were less so. The local police constable offered his own version of events:

PC Pearce, Llwynypia, stated that the pond to the brink of which the ghost carried Mrs Dunn is about 300 yards away from the cottage. He had been telling Jack, the husband, that the noise he heard in the house at night was not produced by a ghost, but it was no use arguing with Jack, because it only drove him out of temper. The delusion had stuck in Jack's mind, and also in his wife's and neighbours' brains. A very large number of people had visited the premises, and remained outside the house until a late hour in the evening. Dr Jennings had also visited the premises, and described the whole affair, according to PC Pearce, as a pack of nonsense. But the matter is, nevertheless, the topic of the day in the district, and has caused a great sensation among the residents.

Police Sergeant Hoyle went even further in distancing himself from the report, and wrote to the paper claiming that he was never there in the first place:

> While reading a copy of your paper this morning I came across my name in connection with the ghost story, as having watched the house which is supposed to be haunted for several hours. Now, as I only knew for the first time, through reading your paper, that there was such a thing at Llwynypia, I wish to emphatically deny the statement with regard to my watching the house in question, as neither I nor any of my men have been near the house.

Despite this, Mrs Dunn (who is referred to here as Mrs Downe) remained adamant that it was all true, and submitted an 'Authoritative Version of the Mystery' to the newspaper in which she expanded on the details of the case, and explained the long-term effects of the experience:

> I am the woman who was carried away, and I am the woman who can tell you the truth about it. I have plenty of witnesses who have heard the noise, and I had plenty of company in the house when he (the ghost) took me away. They asked the constable who looks after the company's houses to stop here a night to hear and see, if he could, but he did not come. I was sitting on a chair by the fire, with three other persons – Mrs Lewis, Mrs George, and John Samuel. The company was outside.
>
> It was at half-past eight in the evening, as near as I can say, when the ghost pulled me off the chair towards him to the passage. I was afraid, and I

screamed, and jumped back to my chair. He was still there. Mrs Lewis told me to speak to him. I felt too nervous at first, but after a time I started to speak to him, when, before I could finish my words he pushed me out from the house and across the bailey and into the water closet. Here he lifted me on to the seat, standing, and he pointed to the top of the wall. He told me in Welsh to raise the stone and take what was under it, and that I must go with him. That was all he said to me there.

Then he took me down about 200 yards from the house. I cannot tell you how he took me from the closet because I lost all my control. I found myself by the brim of a pond. Here he took from me what I had in my hand, and threw it into the water. Then he told me he should never trouble me any-more. So that's all the truth, and I hope you'll be so kind as to put the truth down in your paper.

I am not able to do the washing nor anything else; I am not the same woman that I was before, and I don't think I ever will be. I can give you these names and many others who can swear to what I have said – John Samuel, 9, Amelia-terrace; Mrs Lewis, 1, Amelia-terrace; and Mrs George, 11, Amelia-terrace.

Cardiff's Lady in Grey

In October 1893, a correspondent known only as 'Gwen' wrote to the *Evening Express* after experiencing some strange events in the village of Tongwynlais.

It was while visiting a country house owned by a Mr and Mrs Henry Lewis that the 'Lady in Grey' made an appearance, whose activity included wrapping her arm around an unsuspecting victim.

Gwen began by pointing out how unlikely it might seem that 'a ghost, real and genuine, would venture in these cold prosaic days to haunt within a few miles of practical go-ahead Cardiff', before setting the scene:

You know the pretty pale-green stucco house on the outskirts of the village of Tongwynlais, among verdant pastures, and therefrom, doubtless, named 'Greenmeadow.' Can one believe that when the sun has set and twilight shadows deepen into night, other inhabitants than those of earth steal from their lurking places, wherever that may be, and wander through the rooms where once, perchance, in robust health and glowing spirits, they entertained right royally the distinguished assemblies of their little day? Yet, so, indeed, it is.

Down the long passages a woman glides. A woman? No, the shadowy form of a woman, enveloped in a shapeless film of cloudy grey. She sometimes steals along in silence, but, wayward ever in her changing moods, occasionally her high heels (this dame belongs to a period long gone by) sound with a ringing clang, and pass close to the owners or the servants of the house. Yet she remains invisible, conveying only as she goes on her way an indescribable sensation of a 'presence', felt, but not revealed.

She then explains that the best time to catch a glimpse of the ghost is during the 'witching hours', and that the spirit is known to appear:

in a large, old-fashioned bedroom, which overlooks the drive, so situated that it can be entered only through dressing-rooms, one on either side. Often the doors of these ante-rooms are left ajar, closed, or open when the family retires at night, and are found in the morning in a changed position. Friends often sleep in the haunted chamber, sometimes actuated by a desire to see the ghost. But, though she is often 'felt,' she is rarely seen within the sacred precincts of her favourite haunting grounds.

What follows are accounts gathered by Gwen from witnesses who claim to have been in contact with the 'Lady in Grey', and any other spirits which might haunt the house:

Mrs Henry Lewis's mother has often in the night been awakened, when occupying this chamber, by the alarming sensation of a form she cannot see bending caressingly over her. And even when the presence moves away she is still conscious that she is not alone, for garments rustle, soft sighs are drawn, or doors pushed swiftly to, and yet they never bang!

Miss Gwen Lewis (the violinist who gave a concert recently in Cardiff) has also had some experience of the ghost. 'I don't mind,' says Miss Gwen Lewis, bravely, 'how long she wanders about the room, or even bends over me, but I hope it will never develop into an actual embrace.'

Mr Henry Lewis has often been startled with the footsteps, which he remembers hearing very distinctly when he was a boy; and a Miss Vaughan, who for some time occupied Greenmeadow, during a period in which the owners found it convenient to reside elsewhere, was so distressed by the noises of the unseen inhabitants at night that she had a strong doorway built and placed at the entrance to the haunted portion of the house, which, in some measure, deadened their sounds of revelry and mirth.

The servants have borne witness to seeing many strange figures, among others a little man in red, but upon these I shall not enlarge, but keep my narrative strictly within bounds of authenticated accounts.

The final 'authenticated account' was narrated to Gwen by the lady of the house herself, Mrs Henry Lewis:

One night, a lady who was staying here and I were about to retire, when, recollecting what an excellent housekeeper she prided herself upon being, I suggested that we should take a peep at my storeroom. My thoughts were extremely practical. I wondered why my housekeeper had been so careless as to leave the key of the storeroom in the door; and, having pointed out my pots of jam, &c., my quick eye detected another proof of servants' carelessness, a mere trifle, but still an extravagance, the window sash had snapped, and they had recklessly taken a new brush to prop the lentil with – I tell you these details that you may understand how very far from ghosts and sentiment were all my thoughts – when, stepping forward to see if there were not some less useful article handy which would suit the purpose until a carpenter could be called in, I was a little surprised to find my friend, as I thought, pass her arm round my waist and draw me affectionately towards her.

I turned my head naturally towards her – to find that what I felt I could not see – my friend was facing me at the other side of the room! Drawing myself out of the weird embrace with a moan of terror, I alarmed her so much that, dreading a fit of hysterics, I muttered some broken words about 'a mouse.' Unfortunately, my friend had the greatest horror of mice, and was terribly agitated at the thought of having been in such close proximity to one, dreaded lest she had brought it upstairs in her skirts, until at last to calm her I told her the truth. Then she was quiet at once.

'A ghost,' she said reverently. 'Oh, if I had only known how glad I should have been. A ghost is an honoured treasure in a family – a relic of the past to be revered – and you deceived me with the cruel suggestion of a vulgar little mouse.'

The strangest part is yet to come. I found sometime afterwards that my housekeeper, who, of course, knew nothing of my experience, had been so alarmed by the apparition of a woman in grey gliding along just as she fixed the key in the storeroom door that she took to her heels and fled, and could not be persuaded to return and lock the door.

At this point, Gwen asks Mrs Henry Lewis if she believes in clairvoyance, to which she relates another 'very strange experience':

When first Mr Lewis brought me home to Greenmeadow I was accompanied by two maids, who were devoted to me, and between one – Phoebe – and myself an affection existed, rarely found nowadays between mistress and maid. Phoebe married, and, having settled in a cottage in the village, often came to see me. I was very ill on one occasion, and she stayed with me until about ten at night, when, knowing I was surrounded by professional care, she left me to go home. Only a few minutes later I was subjected to a terribly severe attack, my life seemed fleeting, and as the nurse approached me, 'Phoebe,' I whispered, 'Phoebe.' Now, Phoebe when she reached home and was about to undress turned to her bed, and saw me lying prostrate there. 'Phoebe,' she heard me whisper, 'Phoebe,' and, throwing on her cloak, she came back to Greenmeadow and burst in upon Mr Lewis in great excitement, fearing I was dying. Don't you think that was very strange, indeed?

A rival to Hamlet's father

A ghost, which was described as a 'rival to Hamlet's father', made an appearance at a residential home in Swansea in 1895.

In William Shakespeare's play the ghost delivered a prophecy from beyond the grave, and his competitor appeared to do the same in Wales. And while the reporter covering the case concluded by stating that they believed the story to be a scam, what is noteworthy about this haunting is that it was investigated by the police, and that it did result in the discovery of hard evidence following a tip-off from the spectre – that of buried skeletal remains in the garden.

The events took place in the home of Caroline Bond of 3 York Street, 'a small dingy little place hardly long enough for a decent-sized ghost to move in', and began with the initial report of an inhabitant being 'startled out of their senses by nocturnal visits from what one old lady described as a "ghastly ghost"'.

Our reporter starts by describing the incident, along with a slightly unflattering description of the lady who raised the alarm:

Mrs Bond is a married woman about 40 years of age, and in appearance does not seem to be the sort of creature that would be easily frightened by her own shadow or anything that a vivid imagination could bring before the mind's eye. On the other hand, Mrs Bond is a plump, matter-of-fact, practical, not-easily-to-be-frightened woman, who would scorn the idea of a ghost being in her back kitchen or garden unless it was there in the form of flesh, bone, and muscle. But that is another story. What we are chiefly concerned about is that five minutes after midnight on Tuesday evening last when Mrs Bond was sitting in her kitchen.

Suddenly she heard a strange, rustling noise as of someone coming down the stairs in light indiarubber boots. Glancing furtively round she was horri-fied to find some strange weird spectre standing behind her, and beckoning her to follow into the garden. The ghost opened the kitchen door, and disap-peared in the blackness of the night. Mrs Bond preferred the warm, bright glow of the fire and refused to follow.

But this first encounter wasn't to be an isolated incident. At precisely the same time on the following night – 'ghosts are punctual' – there was a repeat performance:

The unwelcome stranger appeared again, and with a majestic wave of the hand beckoned Mrs Bond once more to follow. She wasn't having any, and shook her head as a sign of her disinclination. The 'ghost', being unsuccessful in its second attempt, dropped its jaw and appeared quite broken-hearted. In spite of the cold and the wet the apparition went out again and Mrs Bond heaved a sigh of relief that the visitor had not asked for a night's lodging. This second appearance quite unnerved her, and when she tried to rise from her seat she felt herself held down by some unearthly spell. She shivered so terri-bly and was unnerved so completely that for the moment she seemed beside herself, and to have awakened from some strange, hideous dream. Throughout that night sweet slumbers kept away – the bedroom seemed full of the ghoul-ish fraternity 'yawning, gaping, and fuming,' so she says.

On the third night Mrs Bond was prepared for her visitor, and recruited her husband and a 'big bunch of her bravest neighbours' to lie in wait:

The ghost arrived ten minutes late – it had probably been detained some-where – but this brave little band of York Courters were waiting for it, breathless, anxious, and excited. About a quarter past twelve o'clock the silence grew deadlier. Suddenly there seemed to be someone tapping, 'gently tapping,' at the door, as Edgar Allan Poe has it. Then was the hair of all dis-turbed as they whimpered with bated breath to each other, 'The ghost, the ghost!' And so it was. The hollow cavernous voice as of one coming from a far country was familiar to Mrs Bond. She nudged her neighbours, and warned them solemnly to be in readiness. The next moment the scene was changed. Strong men turned pale, the women shrieked and the children clutched their mothers convulsively. The ghost was in their midst and bade the company follow into the garden.

There is no obedience so implicit as that which is the product of terror and fright. At least such was the case this night, for the weakest were the first to follow. The night was dark, and the goblin stood a few paces off the crowd, pointing with a long, bony forefinger to a spot in the garden. All eyes were riveted on that spot and the ghost for 'five long minutes.' The spirit seemed to exercise the same influence over their optics as that of the snake over the bird, or other ghosts over a much-soaked tippler. At last, suddenly, the spectre of the night disappeared without having even wished them 'Good night.'

It is at this point that the reporter draws a parallel between the events in Swansea and the scene from *Hamlet*, which leads to an unexpected discovery:

There was much that reminded one of the play, and the similarity was ren-dered more striking when one of the men present took unto himself a shovel *a la* the grave digger, and commenced to dig the earth at the spot which the ghost had indicated. The company formed themselves into a circle and opened their eyes wider as each spadeful of earth was removed. Then the shovel struck something which was not a stone. The moon just then peeped from behind a cloud and shed its refulgent rays on a skull – a human skull! Great Scott! The blood of the beholders turned cold. One man stooped warily, and, grasping the smooth, rounded brain-box nervously, and moved by what he had previously seen, or heard, muttered *'Alas, poor Yorick, I knew him well.'* The party then dispersed in solemn silence.

The matter was passed into the hands of the police, who kept the skull in Swansea's Guildhall. And it was only later that 'one sober fact' came to light

– it was not a human skull, but that of a dog. With this new development in the case, the reporter returned to York Court for a night-time vigil in order to uncover the truth. And immediately upon entering he suspected something was amiss, finding himself at the centre of attention for 'scores of wicked twinkling eyes, mostly those of females, and in front and behind there was continuous giggling and laughing, which confirmed the theory that the whole thing was a hoax – a very funny hoax'.

He noticed Mr Bond near the 'grave' with a gimlet in his hand, and the mystery, as far as the reporter was concerned, would soon be closed:

Before I had spoken half-a-dozen words, Mrs Bond came out, and in a most inviting way I asked her 'is it true; do you now say that you saw the ghost?' 'Come into the house,' angrily exclaimed Mr Bond to his better half, 'I have had quite enough or this business,' and like the 'ghost,' both disappeared. It seems pretty clear that there has been a good deal of yarning about the ghost and the skull of the poor dog.

3

TALKING WITH
THE DEAD

*That there are real communications from 'the beyond,' or 'the unseen,' or 'ghost land,'
or whatever we may call it, there seems to be no room for doubt. Almost every person
must have had some experience in their lifetime sufficient to establish the fact, though
not to explain the cause.*

The more things change, the more they stay the same.

From the mystic druids of ancient times to the celebrity psychic mediums of the twenty-first century, for as long as there have been human beings on this earth, it would seem, there have been those among us who claim to be able to communicate with the dead.

In the Victorian era, the spectacular rise of spiritualism saw everyday people attempting to interact with their dearly departed like never before. Unusual tales of séances, which had been popularised in America by the Fox sisters, who as children had devised a knocking system to 'speak' with a spirit in their family home, were winging their way across the Atlantic. Introduced to British soil by American medium Mrs Maria Hayden in 1852, their popularity was bolstered further by such media darlings as Scottish medium Daniel Dunglas Home.

A typical séance would involve participants sitting around a table, hands touching, in the presence of a medium who might be able to channel a spirit while in a trance. There were various methods of communication, including table turning, which would result in the table tipping and rotating in answer to questions, and spelling out the alphabet (later simplified as a spirit board, or the commercially branded Ouija board) in order to receive more specific replies.

But knocks and letters weren't the only means of communication – spirits could also be seen, heard, smelt and felt.

The increasingly fantastical séances, in which musical instruments were inexplicably played and full-bodied apparitions emerged from closets, naturally drew scepticism from some quarters. Unbelievers predicted that such 'nonsense' would soon be a thing of the past, and at a lecture at Barry Literary Society, Dr Percy Smith, an open-minded paranormal enthusiast, gave the following damning verdict:

> It is, perhaps, not too much to say that the history of modern spiritualism has been in the main a history of impudent fraud and astonishing gullibility. We are not justified in concluding that there is nothing in spiritualism, but until spiritualists are prepared to dissociate themselves from those who prefer darkness rather than light, they need not expect level-headed men and women to trouble very much whether they are right or wrong.

On the other hand, spiritualism also had some powerful supporters, including Sherlock Holmes creator Arthur Conan Doyle, American President Franklin

D. Roosevelt, and the inventor of the telephone, Alexander Graham Bell. Possibly the most high-profile Welsh public figure to profess a belief in some of the claims, and to investigate matters further, was Alfred Russel Wallace.

Alfred Russel Wallace from the 1878 edition of *Natural Selection*.

World-renowned for having conceived of the theory of evolution independently of Charles Darwin, the biologist might seem like an unlikely backer of the movement. But having been criticised earlier in his career for experimenting with mesmerism, which was itself closely associated with spiritualism, Wallace was well prepared for any backlash that he might receive. In 1893, he wrote that:

> Nothing has been more constantly disbelieved and ridiculed than the alleged appearance of phantasms of the living or of the recently dead, whether seen by one person alone, or by several together. Imagination, disease, imposture, or erroneous observation have been again and again put forth as sufficient explanation of these appearances. But when carefully examined they do not prove to be impostures, but stand out with greater distinctness as veridical and sometimes objective phenomena.

Wallace stood firm in his beliefs, and despite all of the damning exposés of fraudulent mediums which followed, he insisted that there was some element of truth in the phenomenon for the remainder of his life.

The opinions of the Welsh public on the subject – or rather, those who voiced their opinions via the printed page – also varied, ranging from blind faith to angry disbelief. In 1894, even the *Western Mail*'s level-headed ladies' agony aunt, who answered questions on all 'social, hygienic, decorative, or personal topics', couldn't quite bring herself to dismiss the idea of spiritualism. When asked 'Do you believe in spiritualism and seeing spirits as they do on Sunday evenings in Queen Street Arcade?' by one reader, she gave the evasive reply that 'There is spiritualism and spiritualism, and I could not answer your question in this column.'

Séances in Wales

What actually happened at a Victorian séance?

For a first-hand account we can turn to William Scott from Merthyr Tydfil, who attended his first gathering in Cardiff in 1877. During the session he heard sounds and saw the manifestations of fully formed spirits, who communicated with him through speech and writing.

But the highlight was the surprise appearance of a deceased relation, which left the narrator in no doubt about the medium's powers. His account of the evening follows:

Having had occasion to visit Cardiff on Wednesday, the 26th of December, I called the same evening on Mr Lewis, Roath, and asked him if he would kindly allow me to attend one of his séances. He consented to my doing so on the following Thursday, at six o'clock pm. On entering the séance room I was introduced to several persons, all strangers, with the exception of the worthy host. I was asked to search the medium, who is a delicate and unassuming young man. I felt a delicacy in doing so; however, on their insisting I acceded to their request, and found nothing on him but his ordinary wearing apparel. I also carefully searched the cabinet, which is a kind of closet at the back of the room in which we sat. At the same time, I was far from mistrusting anything that was sanctioned under the roof of such a gentleman, whose honesty, uprightness, and love of truth is unquestionable.

We sat with the gas burning sufficiently to enable anyone to read. After the usual service (singing and reading a prayer), the medium was entranced by a spirit, whom the company said was called Twilight. He then entered the cabinet under control, at the same time the harmonium was played upon by a gentleman. In about ten minutes or a quarter of an hour a materialised spirit came out into our midst and touched the harmonium and also the player. In the course of the evening I witnessed as many as nine materialisations, each of them different in form and appearance, and, as regards height, from six feet one and a half inches to a baby child. A lady spirit stood outside the cabinet purporting to be the first wife of the late Robert Dale Owen, of America. I spoke to her, telling her at the same time that I admired the writings of her husband, and asked her if she would write me something as a souvenir of this remarkable séance. She said 'Yes,' and advancing towards the table a distance of two or three feet from the cabinet, she took some note paper which was lying on it, and wrote me three pages full in the gaslight, and folded the paper and gave it me, which I have now in my possession.

Near the conclusion of the séance a spirit, who was called Hopeful, said there was a spirit child with him who wished to materialise. This being the first attempt, a gentleman asked the name. The spirit said 'Florey Scott,' who was my little girl who died about eight years ago. I saw her come out of the cabinet, and heard her say, 'I am here, papa; I can materialize.' Now, sir, I wish to draw your attention to this fact, that not one person in that room knew that I ever had a daughter of that name. Many other things took place which are worthy of record, but I fear I have trespassed too much already on your kindness.

The touch of deathlike fingers

In the following report from 'Clearstone', who attended his first séance in Swansea in 1879, the activity witnessed included 'the mysterious tappings and tiltings of tables, the gyrations and tintinnabulations of tambourines, the wandering sifflements of ghostly whistles, the evanescent play of phosphorescent lights and – O horrible, most horrible! – the shivery contact of cold and clammy hands.'

Yes, the shivery contact of cold and clammy hands – ghosts could physically interact with the living.

Before attending the séance, our narrator noted that he had read much about spiritualism and went along more out of curiosity than in search of any real evidence of an afterlife. But what might have been intended as a fun night out proved to be far from a laughing matter when 'deathlike fingers' searched in the darkness, causing the ladies to shriek and faint. He recalled the evening for the local press:

A fortnight ago, a friend asked me to his paternal parlour, to meet a select party of bodies – and spirits. Gladly, if somewhat timidly, accepting the invitation, I spent some time in cogitating upon the probabilities – the dread possibilities! – of that promised apocalyptic evening. What should I see – hear – feel? Oh-h-h-h-h! The thought was shudderingly overpowering.

But the evening has arrived. There are some ladies to be called for – a task congenial enough in general, but tonight…! Small-talk won't flow. Solemn thoughts will clothe themselves in solemn words, until the merry little maidens themselves catch the contagion, and half withdraw from the ordeal. Do we believe in spiritualism? Well, that is the question direct, which one would rather not answer. Even though there should be a mysterious force, is it necessarily connected with the souls of the departed?

There was nothing extraordinary about the back-parlour, or about the Pembroke table round which the company sat with open hands flat on its surface in the full gas glare. Now, all laughter and tittering must cease. Let us compose our minds to seriousness, and elongate our faces. Are there any good spirits here tonight? Thump, goes the table three times, in token of 'Yes'. One thump is to mean 'No', and two thumps, 'Doubtful'. What will the good spirit tell us? O, what we like. Will it tell the ages of the ladies? (Commotion among the ladies.) Flip, flap, flop! goes the table with an alacrity of ungallantry which would lead to the belief that the rapping was done by the spirit of some dear departed old maid.

Is Mr A in love? was the next question prompted by an interesting and interested young girl. Mr A frowned, looked convicted, blushed slightly, but the table replied doubtful, to the general relief of the ladies present. And so the light séance went on, the table talking to its interrogators, with great volubility of rapping, and flopping, and tilting. But why doesn't it sometimes tilt the other way? asks an anxious inquirer. It will sometimes, says the chairman. Will it now? Doubtful, says the table; and it would not tilt the other way. Having exhausted the list of questions which the company had to put respecting things past, present, and future, and having received responses that left the party not much wiser than before, the query of queries was ventured, 'Shall we have a dark séance tonight?' and answered in the affirmative.

A dark séance was conducted in – as the name would suggest – the dark. One of the reasons given for the lack of light is that ghosts are more receptive to the blackness, but of course, it could also allow unscrupulous mediums an opportunity to play tricks of their own:

All hands tightly joined on the table, and the gas went out. No fire, no glare through window or keyhole – total darkness! Silence and palpitation of heart! Then arose slowly and softly the strains of an ancient congregational tune in the minor key. As the weird incantation now swelled into fullness of harmony and now sunk in doleful cadence, hark! What was that unearthly jingle? Is it the clanking of ghostly chains as the wicked spirits troop into the chamber? Or is it the shaking of the small tambourine, which we thought we noticed on the sofa before the gas went out? Yes, it is the tambourine, which is now heard to dance about in the upper air of the four corners of the room, as if grasped in the unsubstantial hands of some Cachucha-dancing sprite. O, the terror of that presence! Then the tambo descends and lightly bumps us each on the head, and the ladies shriek in accompaniment. Then within the dense darkness is seen to rise a dimly phosphorescent light, that quickens and dies and lives again, and alights on the nose of a young lady, and whisks away to the ceiling, quicker than electricity, and so, after a hundred curious and inexplicable pranks, goes out as it came in, 'almost quite too awfully' noiselessly.

But this is no time for gratulation. The horrors of the séance are accumulating thickly upon us. After the aerial meanderings of tambo and 'corpse candle,' comes 'the touch of a vanished hand.' Bob, bob your heads, all ye instructed ones, even bob them down in the darkness, for there is now going forth through the grim atmosphere of the chamber a cold clammy hand, whose deathlike fingers search for your faces, to pat your head in kindliness, to box your ears in wrath, or to pull your nose in ignominy. It comes; it is coming; it is here. Heugh-h-h! This is past human endurance. One lady has fainted, all of them are shrieking for pity and for light, dear light. Hands have been all the while held in remorseless grip, as that other hand felt for its victims, but now are they wrenched asunder with terrified cries, and the séance is broken up in disorder. The ignited gas reveals pale and fearful faces of ladies, and one in a faint. There is sprinkling of water, and coming to, and shivery, shuddery solemnity for the remainder of the evening.

They who only read may laugh, but they who went through the mystic ordeal do anything but giggle, when, in the dead of night, the memory of the tambo dins in their ears, and the icy cold hand pulls their sleepless nose.

Spirit faces by candlelight

In some of the more memorable séances recorded, the spirits weren't just heard and felt, but seen. Despite the darkness of the setting, spirit forms could at times be glimpsed moving around the room, ranging from phosphorescent lights and ethereal hands to full-bodied apparitions of recognisable individuals.

Of them all, the most convincing manifestations were those where a face could be distinguished, which allowed séance-goers to identify their loved ones and other personalities.

In 1873, *The Medium and Daybreak*, a weekly periodical 'devoted to the history, phenomena, philosophy, and teachings of spiritualism', reported one such case from a public séance with the mediums Mr and Mrs Holmes.

A small group of people had gathered for the occasion, consisting mainly of 'those who had sat before at Mrs Holmes's séances', and what follows is an account of the evening's proceedings:

The evening commenced with the usual dark séance, which was of a very pleasing and successful description. Instruments were carried and played by the spirits, and the sitters were touched repeatedly with them.

The spirits 'Richard' and 'Rosie' came round the circle speaking in an audible voice, and touching the hands, heads, and faces of the sitters quite freely. Mr Corin, of Swansea and Cardiff, was slapped on the head by 'Richard,' the concussions being so loud as to be heard all over the room. 'Rosie' kissed a lady present, and the ring was put on a gentleman's arm who had never witnessed any of the phenomena before. The dark séance being finished, arrangements were made for the spirit-faces.

One-half of the folding-doors leading into the back drawing-room was opened, and a temporary door of leather cloth substituted, which had an aperture about a foot square and five feet from the floor. The back drawing-room being thoroughly searched, and the doors locked, Mr and Mrs Holmes sat in front of the temporary cabinet, and in full view of the spectators, with a small table between them; the visitors forming part of a circle, commencing behind Mr Holmes and extending in a curve in front of the aperture. Two candles were left burning at the left-hand side of the room, but they were shaded by a newspaper being placed in front of them to prevent the rays from falling directly on the aperture. Ultimately one of the candles was extinguished, as the rays crossing each other interfered with the experiment. There was, however, plenty of light to see every object quite distinctly.

In a little while a face appeared at the opening, the features of which were indistinct and ghastly. This face was not recognised. The second presentation was that of an old man, with prominent, shaggy eyebrows, strong aquiline nose, and prominent chin. This form was recognised by a lady present as the well-known features of a spirit whom she frequently sees in the clairvoyant state. Mr Burns, who has received many communications from this spirit, asked if the figure represented the spirit alluded to, when it nodded in the affirmative. The next face was that of a diminutive little girl, of small features, but exquisite form. Mrs Burns at once recognised it as a sister who died in childhood, as she was exceedingly small in figure and deficient in vital power. It is the same spirit that appears on a spirit-photograph obtained by Mrs Burns at Mr Hudson's. These identities have been certified since by communications from the spirit thus represented. After this an old lady with a cap on appeared at the opening. A lady present thought she recognised the figure as bearing a likeness to a deceased relative, and the strange gentleman was impressed that it was the likeness of his grandmother, whom he well remembered, but the features were too indistinct to be successfully recognised.

The last face that appeared was the most perfect form of the whole series, and remained longest in view. It was that of a man, apparently of large build, and upwards of sixty years of age. The hair was of a dark iron grey colour, considerably mixed with black, and parted on one side. The brow was square and massive; the nose rather high and sharp; with a well-formed mouth and white beard. Mr Corin, who sat next to Mr Burns, at once exclaimed that it was his father, every feature of whose likeness was strikingly portrayed in the object before him. Mr Corin was deeply interested in what he saw, so much so that for a few seconds he felt so absorbed that he could not speak to the spirit. He then addressed him, and asked if it was indeed his father, when the figure made signals in the affirmative. This form lingered for a long time, showing the face in various aspects, going away and coming again. There could not be a more successful instance of identity than this was. After this figure appeared, the power was exhausted, and the séance terminated, everyone being highly gratified with what had been witnessed.

The language of heaven

Spirits at séances weren't always restricted to the English language.

In 1895, a séance in London took on a distinctly Welsh feel when a ghost appeared to communicate in the Welsh language in order to make contact with one of his countrymen. The reporter noted that:

> although it may not be universally admitted outside the Principality that Welsh was the language spoken in the Garden of Eden, it seems to be indisputable, from the evidence of a spiritualistic séance, that it is one of the tongues, if not the only language, used in the spirit world.

The spirit summoned 'from the vasty deep' said his name was John King, and what follows is an account of events by 'a Welshman':

> He asked my name. I told him it was Thomas. He said, 'You are a Welshman.' I answered, 'Yes.' He replied, 'Duw a'ch bendithio (God bless you). Give me your hand.' I gave it to him. As soon as this was done, he told me to stand up. 'Come up,' he said; and I stepped on to a chair first, and then on to the table. I can reach seven feet from the floor, but the hand was still drawing me up. 'Can't you come higher?' he asked. I said 'No.' I was told that he was giving me this special test because I was a Welshman. My hand felt at the time as if there were a thousand pins in it, and for many months after.
>
> Now, King greeted me in the Welsh language, so I asked him if he remembered the Lord's Prayer in Welsh. He at once said, 'Ein Tad, yr hwn wyt yn y nefoedd (Our Father, who art in heaven)'. The pronunciation was perfect in every word. Spirits then played to us on the guitar the tune, 'Ar hyd y nos (All through the night)', a favourite tune with us Welshmen. Then I remember no more.

The reporter ended by remarking that if 'the guitars played in real Cymric, the language may be worth learning in view of future use', along with a light-hearted quip that 'surely the narrator made a mistake in the instruments. They must have been Welsh harps.'

4

THE VICTORIAN
GHOST HUNTERS

They might ask, 'Have you seen a ghost?' What if he never did, that did not prove that there were no ghosts. He had never seen a murder, but that did not prove that there were no murders committed. He had never seen a Fijian, it did not therefore follow that there were no Fijians.

While the reports of ghost sightings during the Victorian era might have caused some to run for safety or cower under their bed covers, there were braver souls who actively went in search of the supernatural – in the name of science, journalism, entertainment, or simply to debunk them.

One of the most pivotal moments in the history of paranormal investigation was the formation of the Society of Psychical Research (SPR) in Cambridge in 1882, whose stated purpose is to 'understand events and abilities commonly described as psychic or paranormal'. The non-profit organisation, which continues to this day, was the first of its kind in the world, and conferred a level of respectability onto a subject which was generally mocked by scientists.

Shortly after its establishment, founding committee members Edmund Gurney and Frederic W.H. Myers wrote to the editor of the *Western Mail* to appeal for any reports from Wales from 'trustworthy sources':

Readers may possibly be aware that a society, entitled the Society for Psychical Research, has lately been established, under the presidency of Professor Henry Sidgwick, for the purpose of inquiring into a mass of obscure phenomena which lie at present on the outskirts of our organised knowledge. It is an object of this society to get hold of as much first-hand evidence as possible bearing on such real or supposed phenomena as thought-reading, clairvoyance, presentiments and dreams, noted at the time of occurrence and afterwards confirmed; unexplained disturbances in places supposed to be haunted; apparitions at the moment of death, or otherwise; and of other abnormal events, hard to classify at present, but which may seem to fall under somewhat the same categories as these. Should any of your readers, now or at any other time, be able and inclined to send us an account, or put us on the track, of any phenomena of the kind which may have come under the cognizance of themselves or their friends, they would greatly oblige us, and would also (as we think we may fairly say) be rendering a real aid to the progress of knowledge in a direction where such aid is much needed. Nothing will, in any case, be printed or published (either with or without names) except with the full consent of the persons concerned.

As was to be expected, in Wales, as with the rest of the United Kingdom, the SPR were met with ridicule by some, with one correspondent in the *Carmarthen Journal* writing that 'The Psychical Research Society has not, we fear, the ghost of a chance of catching its ghost.'

Be that as it may, the SPR did investigate in Wales, with one of the more unusual reports from Cardigan in 1895 claiming that the society would be looking into a case of a spectral animal:

> A farmhouse near Cardigan has the reputation of being haunted. The ghost
> – so a clergyman states, and he tells it gravely – is that of a calf which comes
> into the bedroom, bites at the pillow, and disappears. A minister of the Corph
> (Calvinistic Methodist) went to live there, and it was thought he would lay
> the ghost, but he has given it up. A member of the Psychical Society is going
> to take the case (not the pillow-case, but the case of the calf) in hand.

But the SPR weren't the only people in search of the truth, with curious Welsh investigators also on the hunt for answers.

A call for scientific investigation

Anyone in Victorian times who publicly argued that the supernatural should be taken seriously and investigated by scientists ran the risk of being ridiculed, as some members of the pioneering Society for Psychical Research found out for themselves the hard way.

But in 1990, Henry White, a councillor from the Cathays district of Cardiff, was willing to put his reputation on the line in the local press when he urged for 'scientific investigation' into reports of haunted houses.

The open-minded councillor told the *Evening Express* that the matter had 'long been upon his mind', and that further enquiries should be made into the paranormal 'provided always that the witnesses are witnesses of truth, that the evidence is above suspicion, and that the phenomenon deposed to has the quality of verisimilitude'.

He argued that if inexplicable events were commonplace and accepted in the Bible, why should the nineteenth century be any different? And that:

> since the spiritual manifestations were quite common in scriptural times, what
> is to hinder their appearance now? In other words, if we have had the ghosts
> we may have them again; and, by the same token, who can say otherwise?
> Ghosts were never popular – jests and gibes have ever been hurled at their
> devoted heads by an irreverent and unbelieving world. When you have the
> evidence of men of high culture who affirm belief in spiritual manifestation

it requires a somewhat courageous man to say they are absolutely wrong to demonstration.

To discuss the matter further, an interview was arranged at Councillor White's premises in St Mary Street, during which he spoke of an incident in the Cardiff area which he believed merited further investigation. What follows is his account of the occurrence:

I own several cottages in Merthyr Street, Cathays, two of which are now vacant, numbers fifteen and seventeen. On Saturday last a young girl named Stephens came to me and said her father was desirous of taking a house. I proceeded to make the usual inquiries as to the prospective tenant, and I elicited the fact that her father is now engaged with Messrs Valentine Trayes and Co., timber merchants, of Cardiff. I asked Miss Stephens where her parents resided, and she named another house in the immediate neighbourhood. She further informed me that her parents had only resided in the house as from the preceding Monday, which rather astonished me, and I then asked the very pertinent question as to why her parents desired so quickly to remove to another house. She gave an astounding answer – that the house in question was haunted.

I was naturally astonished. I asked her to inform me as to the character of the supernatural manifestations, to which she replied that they consisted of a series of knocks, which were heard in the wall dividing the front bedroom from the second bedroom, and the aforesaid knocks followed immediately after her parents had retired to rest. She further said that they first heard a series of knocks, followed by a single knock. I suggested that if the house were haunted it was evidently by the spirit of some deceased person, who desired to at once act up a code of signals, in order to communicate with the outer world. I then suggested to Miss Stephens that the neighbours on either side might possibly have been playing a joke, but that she indignantly repudiated, saying that the neighbours in both houses had been questioned, and they positively stated that they had not been the cause of the noises referred to. She repeated that the knocks were loud and distinct, and that they could not be accounted for by any natural means.

I further asked her if she had made any inquiries as to the antecedents of the persona living in the house in question, and she said her parents had been informed that at one time a woman who lived in the house either poisoned herself or some other person. I suggested that in the circumstances the matter should certainly be further investigated, but she seemed to have a horror of pursuing the subject, and added that her parents were anxious to quit the house as soon as possible. Hence her application. I told Miss Stephens that if her father would bring me, as a matter of business, a reference from his present employers I should be very pleased to further entertain his application for the house. I should add, in conclusion, that Miss Stephens appeared to be a girl of from eighteen to twenty; that she is very intelligent, and that she certainly seemed to be impressed by the truth of her representations to me.

Having heard the story, Councillor White decided to pay a visit to the supposedly haunted house, and presented the findings of his investigation:

> The manifestations are heard only at the stroke of midnight. The present tenants have been in the house a fortnight, those before them a month, and the people before that only a week. They all heard the noises.
>
> The ghost has never been seen. Had the story been concocted it would have been seen many times. But the noises are there still, and, whatever the cause, the phenomenon opens up a field of inquiry for the Psychological Society.
>
> The witnesses are trustworthy; the evidence is above reproach; such manifestations, with our knowledge of the past, are antecedently probable; and, if a man may not believe in ghosts because he has not seen them, upon what ground can he be blamed for refusing to accept a lot of other things which also he has not seen?

Looking to the future, the councillor proposed a plan of action for further investigation, as well as some practical guidelines for any would-be ghost hunters who might want to join in with the evidence gathering:

> As a preliminary step, each of a party of friends associated with a common object should take one of these books (he suggests a book called *The Medium* and other volumes giving information about the matter) and thoroughly digest its contents and make notes upon it. Then a conference should be held, notes compared, and views interchanged, and, finally, it should be determined to pursue a course of systematic investigation, the whole thing to be followed up, if possible, to some real conclusion. The movement, of course, should be set on foot with the mutual compact or declaration that the whole of the investigations be thoroughly honest, conscientious, and honourable.

Off with her head

While many of the stories collected in this book might have been terrifying to those who witnessed the strange events, very few of them contain threats of actual bodily harm. But when the *Weekly Mail*'s 'Special Reporter' went to investigate strange happenings in Cwmbran in 1884, he encountered a 'supernatural visitor' who not only tapped and whistled, but threatened to cut off a young lady's 'bloody head'.

He begins his account by setting the scene:

> Cwmbran is excited. In all parts of the village discussion is rife on the probabilities of some supernatural visitations which are reported to have been recently made to the residence of Mr Place, blast manager of the works. Having heard various statements on the subject, I made it my duty last night to make personal inquiries into the matter.

And so it was that, one dark September night, he set off in search of the truth:

> The moon withheld her light, and the only indication that Cwmbran was neither dead nor sleeping was an occasional flickering from a cottage window. Under these circumstances, and imbued with a calm and curious spirit, I pursued my inquiries.
>
> I had previously learnt that at a late hour in the evening numbers of the villagers formed themselves into groups and visited the house of Mr Place in order to attest the truth of the rumours, and with a desire to make myself 'one of the crowd' I kept my eyes open for the likely parties. I failed to find any, and was consequently obliged to hire a guide in the person of a youth I picked up near the station, and wend my way with him along circuitous paths – including canal paths and muddy lanes – to Mr Place's residence, which is situated about three hundred yards beyond the blast furnaces, in a rather lonely part of what the villagers are pleased to call 'the suburbs.'
>
> The house adjoins two or three others, and bears the appearance of being a highly desirable and comfortable place of residence. The current story is that periodical visits are made to the rear part by the spirit of a man dressed in a black coat and vest, a wideawake hat, and moleskin trousers. The form in which it is said to manifest its presence is by tapping at the kitchen window, and blowing a whistle. These manifestations have been frequent, but by only

two persons – a female servant and a policeman – has the form been seen. Regarding the matter superficially, I was inclined, with others, to treat the matter as a kind of hoax, and to think that the servant and the policeman had been fooled by a 'follower.' The searching inquiries I made somewhat changed my mind.

The reporter, putting aside his initial scepticism, then relates the facts to date:

It seems that the supernatural visits have been going on for the past three years, and that, although until recently no decided action has been taken by the occupier of the house, they have caused him considerable annoyance. Three or four months ago he engaged a new servant – a somewhat dull and ingenuous maid of twenty-six. She, like the subject of Edgar Allan Poe's 'Raven', heard a tapping at the chamber door, and for a time I thought it was that and nothing more. Prompted by curiosity, she one night ventured to peep out, and there, according to her story, she saw the form of a man, as already described. Moved by this new feature of the case, Mr Place sought the assistance of the police. For several nights Police Constable Lawrence watched the premises with a vigilance worthy of a better cause; and on one night – last Wednesday week – about half-past eleven, had his curiosity satisfied by obtaining an ocular demonstration of the rumour.

He stoutly affirms that after hearing the tapping and whistling he actually saw the form of a man approach the window and peer through. With the valour of a policeman he first threw his staff at the object – and then fainted. On recovering, he declared that directly he threw his staff the object vanished. On another occasion he sat up with the servant and awaited the coming of the spirit. It came, and from the outside went through the usual performance. The constable and the girl immediately repaired to the door, where the girl declares that she again saw the form, although to the constable it was invisible.

Now comes a remarkable part of the story. With her hand clasped in that of the constable – 'so the legend runneth; so the old men tell' – she commenced conversing with the spirit.

During this conversation between the spirit and the servant girl, she was asked who she was, to which she replied: 'I am a young woman, and if you want me you must come to me. What do you want?'

The constable, curious to know what was being said, asked the girl what the spirit's reply was: 'He says he wants to cut my b— head off,' replied the girl. 'You won't do anything of the sort,' she continued, 'and if you come here I'll cut yours off.' So ended the séance for the night.

But that wasn't the only report of a ghost in the area, and the correspondent also relates another witness account which again saw the police called to the scene of the disturbance:

> About a month ago a young man came down from London to visit some friends who live in the house adjoining that of Mr Place. He occupied the back bedroom, and about three o'clock one morning was awakened by what he thought was a noise on the roof. Rising up, he saw a form at the window. He immediately sought his revolver, and fired several shots, after which the form disappeared. Upon these statements being bruited about they aroused a great curiosity, and parties began to visit the house at a late hour in the hope of receiving the same ocular proof as the policeman declares he did. It was then Mr Place felt the annoyance and caused the police to interfere.
>
> I should state that, with the object of proving whether the tapping was caused by a corporeal being, the officer one night placed across the window a large board loaded with broken bottles. He felt satisfied that it was impossible to get at the window without removing the board, and causing a loud noise; but still the tapping came, and the whistle blew.

Having gathered the facts the reporter decided to investigate the haunted property for himself, but unfortunately did not witness anything unusual at first hand:

> Prompted by the same curiosity as the villagers, I went to the house and watched anxiously for the spirit. I watched until I began to sneeze, and acting on this timely forewarning of an incipient cold I left. It may be that I was too early or that it was not the spirit's night out.
>
> Anyhow, it failed to appear, and I am, therefore, obliged simply to record what I heard, and not what I saw. I know from my professional experience in courts of law – as a journalist, and not as a member of the legal profession – that this is not evidence, and that an affidavit from the spirit itself would receive the court's – I mean my readers' – most serious attention. Still, I would ask the reader to have some respect for the honesty and veracity of the constable and others from whom I obtained my information, and patiently await further developments.

The secrets of Castell Moel

The engraving of Castell Moel (1740) by the Buck brothers Samuel and Nathaniel,
which inspired the ghost hunt.

In an article published in 1895, a reporter for *The Welshman* in
Carmarthenshire began by bemoaning the fact that local ghost sightings
appeared to be on the decline, and by doing so, recorded some memorable
examples for prosperity:

> In old times nearly every venerable mansion had its ghost, but ghosts are
> now getting very scarce. Fifty years ago, if not at a later period, a male ghost
> used to be seen around the grounds at Ystrad. Among those who saw it was
> the late Mr John Davies, of Alltycnap, who had twice that doubtful pleas-
> ure. We have all heard of the dark gentleman who, after the death of 'Betti
> 'Sia,' the witch, used to visit the cottage in which she formerly lived on the
> roadside beyond Cillefwr. The old people of Carmarthen all remember Ty'r
> Bwci (a house which stood on or near the site of the present Longacre Villa)
> and the female ghost who loved to frequent that place and the lane leading
> up to Cwmoernant. But all these ghosts have apparently retired from public
> life, and even Greencastle, on the Llansteffan Road, once so famous for its
> unearthly visitants, appears to know them no more.

But the ghosts of Greencastle – or to give it its Welsh name, Castell Moel –
who had appeared to have deserted the premises would soon be brought back
to the reporter's attention and inspire a ghostly outing in search of evidence:

> Our attention has lately been turned to Greencastle by an engraving of the
> Brothers Buck, which we had the privilege of borrowing from our good

friend Mr Williams, of the Royal Exchange. The engraving has the following descriptive lines underneath: 'This Castle is about two miles to south-west of Carmarthen on a lofty situation commanding an extensive Prospect of the River Towey. It is also call'd Castell Moel, and is suppos'd to be that which is call'd by Dr Powell in his Continuation of H. Lhoyd's History of Cambria, Humffreys' Castle; It is said to be one of those built by Uchtred, Prince of Merionethshire, A.D. 1138. It is at present in the Possession of Thomas Bludworth, Esq., Published according to Act of Parliament, April 5th, 1740.'

The engraving shows the castle in a state of ruin, not very different from its present condition, although some parts of the walls have since fallen in. On one side is a row of trees running westward, and on the opposite side, running in a contrary direction, is a wall with the top battlemented. A glimpse of Carmarthen and the many windings of the Towy (which appear, by the way, to be rather exaggerated), bearing several full-rigged yachts on its waters are seen in the background. In the distance the tower of St Peter's Church and Carmarthen Bridge, with seven arches, are plainly delineated.

And so it was that, armed with the newly discovered engraving, and with a longing to rediscover the ghosts of old, a team from the periodical decided to pay an after-dark visit to Castell Moel:

The twilight hour was chosen in order to give the outing as much of a ghostly character as possible. Mr Jones, whose family has occupied the place for several generations, received the party very kindly, and with his permission Miss Harte showed them over the old castle, which is really much larger than it looks from the road, without speaking of the outstanding fragments of wall, proving that it was originally a good deal more extensive than would appear at present.

Encouraged by Mr Jones's kindness, one of the visitors before leaving ventured to ask him if the ghosts had quite forsaken the old place. Evidently Mr Jones, for all the weight of his eighty-nine years, retains not only a good deal of manly vigour but a considerable sense of humour as well. His eye twinkled as he smilingly confessed to having heard 'old stories,' but he did not plead guilty to having met any ghosts in his own time. The others present were a little more explicit, and Miss Harte said she had heard, not indeed of the fine lady, but of the old gentleman in a three-cornered hat, who appeared there in the early days of the present century to a female domestic. She believed it was in the time of Mr Jones's uncle, whose name, we believe, was David Thomas.

This was probably as far back as the battle of Waterloo. One of *The Welshman* party mentioned a certain aged man living in Carmarthen (often referred to in our Town Notes as 'Old Inhabitant'), and asked if his mother was not the servant who had seen the ghost. Miss Harte believed it was. She then led the way into an ancient kitchen, where there was an immense open fire-place with a sort of settle on each side. She pointed out where the servant was sitting up late one night with a lover who had come to see her, and told how, on looking out into the middle of the room, both saw the gentleman in his out-of-date attire, including the 'three-cornered hat.'

With their tour of the property concluded, the gang had a new lead to follow in their investigation – Carmarthen's unnamed 'Old Inhabitant', who might be able to shed some light on the tale:

On returning to Carmarthen, the ghost hunters thought it incumbent on them to glean all the particulars which 'Old Inhabitant' could supply. His story was to this effect. He had often heard of the servant and her lover who saw the ghost at Greencastle. He was not sure that his mother was the girl, but thought it might have been so, though his mother had never told him that she was the person. He knew that his mother was a servant at Greencastle as far back as 1817. The present Mr Jones's mother had told 'Old Inhabitant's' mother, he added, that she (Mrs Jones) had seen the man on several occasions, always dressed exactly in the same way. The man, or ghost rather, always wore a three-cornered hat, a swallow-tailed coat with a profusion of buttons on it (apparently silver buttons), knee breeches, silk stockings, and shoes with silver buckles. One day Mrs Jones was making bread, when looking up, she saw the man leaning against the pillar in the middle of the kitchen. Recognising her ghostly visitor, Mrs Jones walked out of the kitchen, and when she looked in at the door a moment afterwards he was gone. Miss Thomas, a sister of Mrs Jones, slept in a bed over the staircase, and one night, when the room was so flooded with moonlight that every object was distinctly visible, Miss Thomas was surprised to see a very beautiful lady, handsomely dressed and wearing on her neck, which was quite bare, a lovely necklace. She had a lot of jewellery about her person. At first the thought of an unearthly visitor did not occur to Miss Thomas at all. She thought some fine lady must have called and entered her room by mistake. In a few minutes, however, she was startled to find that the mysterious lady, who never spoke, vanished like morning mist. Nothing more astonished Miss Thomas than the fact that she felt quite unable to speak while the visitor was in the room. About that time Mrs Jones began to find it very difficult to find servants who had sufficient courage to remain at Greencastle, and 'Old Inhabitant's' mother received a pound or thirty shillings (a great consideration in those days) over the usual wages paid to servants at the time. She stayed on, having plenty of nerve and being 'afraid of nothing.' 'Old Inhabitant' understood that the owner of the property got someone at last to lay the ghosts, and that the operation cost a lot of money, but he was never told how the job was effected. 'Old Inhabitant' remembers his mother often telling how, when she was servant at Greencastle, she could see from the hill there the body of Rees Thomas Rees hanging on the scaffold at Pensarn.

Terrors of the night

The following story contains one of the most incredible and, if to be believed, most shocking accounts to be found in this collection. Not only do the ghost hunters witness full apparitions which interact with each other and re-enact crimes from their time on earth, but a member of the party pays the ultimate price – with their life.

But it's worth noting that what follows is a combination of two separate letters, the first of which was published in the 'Letters to the Editor' section supposedly as fact, while the narrator's subsequent – and much more outlandish – letter was published a week later in the 'Our Story Teller' section. This would suggest that, while the original letter was taken at face value, the newspaper considered the second one to be a work of fiction.

The case begins in January 1887 when ghostly lights are reported at Berllan, a property near Llanfaglan. Amateur investigator John Humphreys from Caernarfon takes it upon himself to explore the incident, and makes it quite clear from the offset that he already had a strong belief in the paranormal. In fact, he was unhappy with the way that ghosts were being perceived at the time as mindless entities, and urged them to put more effort into conveying the true nature of their visitations:

Their appearances generally appear to have resulted only in terrorizing the ignorant or puzzling the learned. This is a grave slur upon the race of ghosts, and it behoves them for the sake of their reputation in this utilitarian age, to achieve some distinctly useful end, else, in spite of the warmest sympathy and support of myself and others, they will finally and for ever come to be regarded as unmitigated nuisances.

Having voiced his personal feelings on the subject, he continues with a recap of all the available evidence to date, and a description of the haunted location, complete with directions for anyone wishing to pay a visit themselves:

Berllan is an empty house about two miles from Caernarfon, after crossing the ferry. If any of our readers desire to visit this place, they will best come at it by a walk along the shore, past the old battery and on to Llanfaglan Church, when any resident will point it out to them. Of course, as is orthodox, ghosts do not appear in the day time, hence it will be necessary to make the visit after sunset. From 'information received,' it seems that the ghosts manifest themselves to the chance passer-by from seven in the evening to between two and three o'clock in the morning. This is satisfactory, inasmuch as first, it is the usual time; and secondly, it adds much to the pleasing terror attendant upon these supernatural visitants. But a serious fault must be pointed out in connection with these manifestations at Berllan. So far, the ghosts themselves, *in propria persona*, have not been seen. The only evidence of their existence which has been vouchsafed is the ghostly illumination of the premises.

This is something, it is true, but the most that can be advanced in its favour is that it is better than nothing. Great possibilities, no doubt, lie couchant in these preliminary displays. Interest is awakened, and attention attracted, and may be, when the affair has thus been sufficiently puffed, we shall be regaled with the most terrifying revelations of (who knows!) hidden crime, or secreted treasure. *This* is what every experienced reader of (George W.M.) Reynolds' stories will look forward to, and it must be admitted that this is what every one of your readers is justly entitled to. This *may* come to pass. Indeed, from a long and deep study of the proceedings of ghostly visitations in all parts of the country, I am confident that this is actually what *will* ensue on the present nightly illuminations of the deserted Berllan, but, till this stage *is* reached the Berllan ghosts ought clearly to understand that they stand discredited in the enlightened community at present residing in Caernarfon. The bare statement of facts respecting our interesting visitors as given below, and I think that even the ghosts themselves will admit that it is nothing to be proud of.

Berllan is an empty house, which has been unoccupied for some time. Recently, a belated traveller was startled to see every window in the house brightly illumined with a ghostly radiance. To this person's indelible disgrace, be it recorded that he incontinently fled, without making the slightest effort to ascertain the cause of the illumination. He, however, mentioned it to several of his friends, and a strict watch was kept (at a safe distance) on several succeeding nights. These vigils, however, were not rewarded, and belief in the countryman's story began to flicker, when it was suddenly corroborated by another witness who had also seen the strange light on another night, and at a different hour. The vigils were thereupon continued with the result that it was indubitably proved that Berllan was nightly (more or less) lighted up with mysterious fires. On New Year's morning, a party of three or four persons returning from town, witnessed the ghostly radiance, and, strong in numbers, advanced to the house. As they approached, however, the light faded, and on their arrival, vanished altogether. This somewhat disconcerted our investigators, and they precipitately retired. On looking back, however, they beheld the old house once more effulgent with light. A hasty consultation resulted in a resolve to make another attempt to fathom the dazzling mystery, and they all advanced again. But, again the lights vanished, and they were left in total darkness. This time, however, they made an effort to get into the house, but found every door locked, and every window fastened.

Thus, then, the case stands at present, and it cannot be said to be in a satisfactory state. Interested in, and partial to ghosts as I am, I feel impelled to make a personal appeal to *these* ghosts to do something worthy of their race. Let them frighten somebody, reveal some dark crime, or point out (even, if it be only to *me*, and in strict confidence), the whereabouts of some vast treasure trove, and then, but not till then, will public sentiment be satisfied.

And so it was that the challenge to the ghosts was laid down, and John decided that it was up to him to discover the secrets of Berllan. He began with an initial daytime reconnaissance of the premises:

I found it to be a low long building, having only one door in the front, and only two windows, one in the front and one at the back. It is a one storey house, that is, all the rooms are on the ground floor. It stands in the middle of a small enclosure, an orchard, which apparently has at one time been carefully kept. The window blinds are drawn, so that it was impossible to see the interior of the building, and, as both windows and door were fastened I could not get into the house. At the end furthest from the road is a stable. There is no communication between the stable and the house, though the end wall of the house forms one side or end of the stables. Similarly at the end of the stable is a pigsty. I ought to state that the back window slides open, moving from side to side (not up and down), and has no catch to it. But it has been effectually fastened inside, by means of a long iron spoon placed in the slot or travelling groove, in such a position that it is impossible to push the casement open. The enclosure in the midst of which the house stands is entered by a gate, which is not locked, being kept close by means of an ordinary latch. Within a hundred yards of the building is Llanfaglan Farm.

With the facts gathered, he enlisted the aid of a companion and his pet bull-dog for a night-time investigation, during which they would uncover much more than just lights emanating from an abandoned house. What follows is his extraordinary account of that fateful night:

I returned to town, fully determined to pay a visit to the haunted house at midnight. Chancing to meet a friend, I mentioned the matter to him, and he at once agreed to accompany me. We decided to keep the *time* (but not the *fact*) of our intended visit to the haunted house secret, from a well-grounded apprehension that if it were known when we were going, the ghosts would not show themselves that night.

On Wednesday night last I determined the trial should be made. As the ghosts have more frequently manifested their presence in the small hours of the morning, it was decided not to set off from town before midnight, and in order to be quite fresh and alert against any possible trickery at the place, I determined to secure a couple of hours sleep before setting off, so, taking an early supper, I lay down about ten o'clock, having arranged to be aroused at twelve sharp.

True to the minute, the night watchman thundered at the door, and, hastily dressing, I hurried off to the ferry to meet my friend. I found him waiting patiently in the boat, a particularly active and ferocious looking bulldog sitting by his side. Jumping in, we pushed off at once, and in a few minutes were well on the way and soon arrived at our destination.

A bright moon fitfully shone over the scene, her splendour being dimmed, and almost extinguished at times by the flying clouds which passed swiftly and thickly across the sky; and a stiff breeze bent the trees and whistled through the hedges with an appropriate ghostly sound. In the stillness of the night we could hear the roaring of the sea on the bar; and every now and again a curlew disturbed by our passage across the fields would rise swiftly, and fly away screaming, in the darkness. Altogether the preliminary incidents were well calculated to prepare our minds for the terrors … but I must not anticipate. As far as I am personally concerned, I am free to admit that I was greatly impressed by the surroundings, but my companion chatted away as cheerfully as usual, his huge cigar glowing in the night as he puffed great clouds of smoke of delicious aroma into the night air, while the stolid brute he had brought with him trotted by his side in characteristic silence.

It may be asked why a dog formed one of our party. Well, we had talked the matter over, and it was thought that, as human beings, we might be more or less tinged with a secret belief in the supernatural, which, in circumstances of unusual excitement, might tend to becloud our reason, and so give a chance to any trickery that might be attempted, to deceive or terrify us. A dog, we thought, especially a *bulldog*, and *more* especially such a complete savage as that now taking part with us in the adventure, would not be affected by anything of the kind which usually passes among the ignorant for something super-natural, and his steadfast courage would serve us as a rallying point for our own, if required. And required it was – but I again anticipate.

Arrived at the place, I must say that I was somewhat relieved to find that the house was in darkness, and I instantly experienced an accession of cour-age and cheerfulness. As we made our way to the house, I loudly informed my friend that the revolver I had brought with me was loaded, and had seven chambers. Then I somewhat vociferously dilated on the ferocity of bulldogs in general, and of that we had the felicity of having with us, in particular. I then ostentatiously complimented my friend on his coolness, his strength, and his well-known courage. And all this I did for the purpose and with the intent of impressing all whom it might concern with the conviction that we were not to be frightened by any ordinary beings. We tried the windows, back and front, and then tried the door. They were all fast. Producing a skeleton key I put it in the lock, turned it, and opened the door. Total darkness confronted us, and for a moment we hesitated. My companion, however, stepped boldly in, I followed, and we closed the door. Then my friend, striking a match, lit a dark lantern and flashed the light over the interior.

We found the house furnished, plainly but comfortably. On our right and left were two doors, one opening into a bed-room, the other into a kitchen and sitting-room combined. The kitchen table was laid out as if for supper, but everything was covered with dust. We examined the whole of the furniture, opened the cupboards, and examined the walls. We found nothing in the cupboards with the exception of the ordinary furniture of such receptacles, and the walls were clearly solid. We then passed into the bedroom. On a table near the bed stood an ordinary paraffin oil lamp. The bed was of the usual kind now in use among the working classes. We glanced at the window and noticed that the blind was drawn. We also noticed that a set of thick curtains were disposed on each side of the window. As we did not wish to let any light we might use pass through the window, we drew the curtains and lit the oil lamp on the table.

Horror! What has happened? The dog, growling, and showing his teeth, retreats backward into a corner, his eyes starting out of his head. Back and back he cowers, horrible human terror depicted on his face. The wall stops his further progress, but he still retreats, cringing before the invisible terror which seemed to be advancing on him. He cowered and shrank to the ground; his menacing growl changed into a gasping choking sound, and still his eyes strained fearfully upward.

The bedroom door opened and closed noiselessly; a cold chill pervaded the room; something had entered, but, whatever it was, we saw nothing, heard nothing. We grasped at each other's outstretched hands, and the contact dissipated our terror. 'What is it?' I asked. 'Get your revolver,' was the reply, 'there's some trickery about.' 'But look at the dog,' I cried. The poor brute was writhing in the corner, twisting his head round as if following the movement of something that was trying to get behind him. 'Give me the revolver,' cried my companion sharply. 'Quick.' At that moment the lamp was suddenly extinguished, and we were plunged into profound darkness; but only for a moment. The heavy curtains we had drawn before the window were thrust aside instantaneously, but with absolute noiselessness, and the rays of the full moon shone brightly into the room. The bedroom door was wide open. We could hear the patter of bare feet: a sound as of someone pacing back and forth through the doorway, as if impatiently waiting the arrival of some expected visitor. Presently the front door opened, and a form entered the room. It was the form of a young woman, who looked carefully into the room, and, apparently seeing nobody, returned on tiptoe to the door and beckoned for someone to enter. We, petrified with terror, watched, certain that some tragic deed would be shown to us. The footsteps we had been listening to had ceased on the opening of the front door.

In answer to the beckonings of the young woman, a man's form entered stealthily and warily, and they moved hand in hand towards the table, passing the window as they did so. Suddenly we saw a phantom arm sweep through the air. It swung with terrible force apparently, and plunged a knife into the breast of the man who had just entered. Without a sound the form of the stricken man sunk to the floor, the knife quivering in his breast. The next moment a burly form sprang from behind the curtain, seized the young woman, and roughly threw her on the body of her murdered companion. Then raising a heavy club, he brought it down with crushing force on her head. To our horror, a dark stream of blood spread over the phantom forms, the blood of the woman mingling with that which flowed from the wounded man, and staining the white floor around us. The murderer gazed wildly for a moment at his bloody work, wrung his hands helplessly, his face frightfully distorted the while. Then, as if stricken with terror, he made a dash for the window, opened it, and made an effort to get through. Instinctively I raised my revolver and pulled the trigger. A deafening report followed, the room was filled with smoke, and the form in the window disappeared. We turned to look at the murdered bodies. They, too, had vanished. We now called to the dog, but no motion answered our calls, and on going to him we found he was stone dead, *his neck broken*. Overcome with terror, we both rushed into the open air. There my companion fainted, while I, calling hoarsely for help, ran to the farm houses close by. I never reached them, however. I had gone but a few steps ere I too reeled and fell, overcome with the terrors of the night.

When I recovered consciousness, I found myself in my own room, lying on the floor, and convulsively clutching the bedclothes.

5

POLTERGEIST
ACTIVITY

The sounds were harrowing as they rose fitfully and at intervals, breaking the silence of the night, and the stoutest nerves among the listeners were shaken.

Poltergeist activity, said to be produced by a disruptive spirit who can cause chaos in the form of noises, damage and levitation, has been reported in different cultures around the world for centuries. But it wasn't until the Victorian era that the word 'poltergeist' itself, derived from the German words *poltern* (to create a disturbance) and *Geist* (ghost), was introduced into the English language to describe a 'noisy spirit' by novelist Catherine Crowe in her influential collection of ghost stories, *The Night Side of Nature* (1848).

Accounts of such activity were reported across Wales at the time, and this example from Holyhead in 1858 details some of the ruin caused by their antics:

> The inhabitants of the vicinity of Cae Drain have been thrown into a state of great consternation by their dwellings being damaged and windows smashed by some invisible agency. Scores of panes of glass have been broken, and stones of various sizes and descriptions are seen hurled at the windows, but, despite the watchful eyes of the neighbours and vigilance of the police force, no clue can be obtained as to the destroyer. The unknown vagabond was carefully watched during the whole of Monday night, but although pane after pane was smashed into atoms, he could not be detected.

Far from an isolated incident, similar reports were on the rise throughout the nineteenth century, and with a new label to describe these far more sinister and destructive entities, all manner of claims were made.

Startling noises down on the farm

Farmyards proved to be something of a favoured target for poltergeists.

Reports from those who lived and worked in these remote dwellings, surrounded by wide, open fields and lonely woodlands, ranged from machinery and items for the home being disturbed and broken, to cattle being set free and, in some cases, even relocated to a different farm altogether.

In this first case from Hafod in the Ystwyth Valley in 1880, a cow was indeed moved to a new location, but that wasn't the supernatural part – it's what came afterwards that was unusual:

> Long before the present handsome mansion was built at Hafod, it appears that the site was occupied by a farmhouse. Ill feeling arose between the tenant of

this farm and a neighbouring farmer. One night the occupier of Hafod took one of his own cows and drove it to his neighbour's farm where he put it in the cow house. Next morning he raised a hue and cry; someone had stolen his best cow. A search was made in several directions, but the cow could not be found. At last suspicion fell on the neighbour. His cow house was searched, and there, indeed, was the stolen animal. In spite of his protestations of innocence he was apprehended.

At the trial which ensued the evidence seemed to be conclusive, and in the end the man was condemned to be hanged. In those days people were hanged for sheep stealing. In course of time, the capital sentence was carried out; but afterwards no one could live in peace at the farm house at Hafod. Nothing appears to have been seen, but during the nights strange noises emanated from all parts of the house, and unseen agencies threw the cheese from the shelves in the dairy, and precipitated other things in different parts of the house to the floor. What became of the tenant, I do not know, but if the ghost worried him into a confession of his misdeed it would be no more than I should expect.

In 1897, 'startling noises which are unaccounted for' were also heard at a farm near the River Wye. The correspondent chose to keep the exact details of the location a secret as 'it would never do for hundreds of people from all parts of the district to be marching some fine day on a mountain farm', but they did vouch for its authenticity, and added that any 'thoroughly worthy inquirers' would be able to obtain the address from the editor. The farm was described as:

> one of those pleasant spots on the Radnorshire hills where the lively imagination can revel in a world of speculation. The side lights of the Wye Valley, trending from the famous river, upland meadows, and hilly cwms redolent of clover and newly-gathered hay, greet you – and yonder, with a belt of roses, isolated and lone, the haunted farm.

What follows is an account of the activity at the unnamed spot, from an informant described as 'a lady of highest worth and respectability', who said that she had no doubt about the validity of the claims of the occupants:

> At T— D—, there have been some peculiar doings. The place is a small mountain farm within sound of the Wye, and up to a short time ago inhab-

ited by an old farmer and his family. For a long time they were troubled with most unaccountable noises, by rappings and movements of the furniture. When it was well known that all the family were downstairs, movements, knocks, and such like were heard in the room above.

They were all out one day last autumn harvesting; the door was locked, and it was beyond dispute that no one could have entered except by breaking the door or window. Yet when they returned from the field they found a condition of things which could only have been done by a sprite of mischief. Every article in the dairy had been taken out and placed in and about the kitchen. The kitchen table was laden. This elfish prank was alternated afterwards by the blankets being drawn roughly from a sleeper's bed. The only variation in the noises was when a married daughter visited the house. Then the rappings became more violent. When she had left they resumed their occasional quiet character and were only heard now and then, but always given so unmistakably that no one doubted that they were supernatural.

The farm is a typical Welsh farm with little that is picturesque save the clusters of roses and the whitewashed surroundings, with trees here and there bent in the direction of prevailing winds. It is not long ago that the old farmer died. The family remain, but have kept the facts to themselves for some time, not caring to talk much about them; but still, they have been thinking of getting a minister there to hold a prayer meeting, and see if the unquiet spirit can be soothed.

Finally, in a case reported in 1889, the police were forced to keep a close eye on Bodurdda Farm, not far from Aberdaron and Bardsey Island, following potentially life-threatening reports of severe damage caused by released cattle running wild:

The inhabitants are thoroughly terrified, and to one of the farm servants the affair is likely to have a serious ending. When the cowman went in early dawn to the shippons to milk the cows, to his astonishment he found the sixteen cows and one bull unfastened in the yard. The bull immediately bolted at the man, knocked him down, thrust his horn right through his cheek, and tore his clothes to tatters, leaving him in a shocking condition. A posse of the Caernarfonshire police were then sent to watch the premises, and during the night three cow-house doors opened simultaneously, and closed with a bang. They rushed out in alarm, but not a soul could be observed, and this extraordinary nocturnal incident has greatly increased the alarm, especially as weird sounds have since been heard.

Strange rappings and stranger fancies

Poltergeist activity wasn't confined to rural locations, and in 1899 'mysterious sounds' were heard simultaneously in two adjacent houses on Cardiff's Riverside Street. It was reported that 'for the last two months unaccountable noises have been heard, and strange rappings have brought stranger fancies into the hearts of the occupants'.

While the author of the article appears to dismiss the sounds as the work of river rats, one of the occupiers was convinced something 'mysterious' was happening, as they described in their account of events:

> For several weeks past I have noticed sounds! It began a few weeks ago early in the morning. At first I took no notice of it, but when I found that it occurred at regular intervals I thought that, perhaps, the neighbours were doing something. They, it seems, had heard it also, and thought that some of my household had caused it. Mutual inquiries led to mutual explanations, but also to mutual alarm, for, whilst on my side we could find nothing to cause the noises, the neighbours next door could find nothing either, and the thing remains a mystery. In my house it sounds as if someone next door knocks with the knuckles against the wall of one of the bedrooms, and when we ask we are told that the noise gives our neighbours a similar impression. At any rate, as we cannot account for it, we are all more or less alarmed, and the affair is being talked about amongst our friends.

One popular theory for poltergeist activity is that it is centred on teenagers, either as an unpleasant and uncontrollable side-effect of reaching adolescence, or as an all-too-human act of juvenile mischief.

In our next account of an urban poltergeist, published in 1894, the investigator was quick to point the finger at the property's young occupant, but by the end of the investigation was at a loss for an explanation:

> It was quite recently at a small town in the hill districts of Wales that a spiritualistic demonstration at a working man's home set the whole neighbourhood in an uproar. A girl, the daughter of a tenant, of the impressionable age of 17, had evidently incurred the displeasure of some revengeful spirits, for they signified their wrath by breaking the crockery and upsetting the utensils in whatever part of the dwelling she remained. My suspicion was aroused when I learned that these frisky demonstrations of demoniacal anger took place

generally in the dark, and always when the girl was alone. The proof of their energy lay in the pile of broken cups and saucers, which the proprietor of the house woefully exhibited to the wondering crowds.

This state of things had gone on for three nights, when I suddenly presented myself at the door, and, as a pressman anxious to cover his journal with glory, demanded that I should be allowed to sit out the night in the haunted kitchen. The ghost, in the course of his antics, had broken the windows, and the crowd outside kept me company, and chattered through the broken panes. I sat there about two hours, and at midnight, when only a straggler or two remained in the street, and I was feeling a bit funky and a trifle tired, when – bang – bang – bang went something in the small kitchen adjoining like someone rapping the table heavily. With the bravery of a forlorn-hope volunteer, I rushed into the room, in time to see in the moonlight a plate falling from a small rough table to the floor, where in the same moment it lay smashed to atoms.

Nobody was there. I searched the room narrowly. I had come through the only door which led into the room, which was really a small washhouse. Not a sign was visible of anyone or anything to account for the banging or the smashing. I confessed myself converted to a belief in the girl's story that she heard similar noises and saw similar things which she could not explain any better than I was able to do. The workman and his family left the house, and the demonstrations ceased. Now, can anybody give a reasonable key to the mystery?

The Woman in White

In January 1897, a ghost story from the Roath area of Cardiff began conventionally enough when 'mysterious knockings' were heard. But after the initial report was published, the volume of evidence escalated as more witnesses came forward with their own experiences.

It all started when the reporter, not particularly acquainted with the paranormal, was sent to investigate the scene of the disturbances:

It is not often that it falls to the pressman's lot to investigate the strange phenomena of the spirit world, but yesterday I went upon an errand of investigation that has opened new possibilities. I began incredulous. I ended it baffled and mystified. The story I tell is a plain unvarnished narrative, and the persons who themselves witnessed the strange sights and heard the strange sounds (as recently as a few days ago) are in Cardiff today and are willing to vouch for the truth of the narrative.

It was told to me by the chief occupant of the house, which, it would appear, is the favourite recreation ground of the disembodied spirit in question, and all the nerve shaking and uncanny experiences set forth below were experienced either by himself or by members of his family. The house in question is situated in Montgomery Street, Roath, not a stone's throw distant from the Recreation Ground. The scene of this story is a newly-built street, a modern brick tenement rejoicing in a tiled floor, slate roof, and stable adjoining.

It sounds prosaic enough in all conscience, and when I visited it and went over it in the broad daylight I must confess I felt a sense of disgust that one of so distinguished a race as had from time immemorial perplexed mankind with unexpected visits should have so degraded itself as to pitch upon so humble an abode, even in a town where the rates are as exorbitant as is the case in Cardiff. Let me say a word at the outset regarding the plan and structure of the house, that my readers may obtain a clear idea of the surroundings amidst which this latest apparition takes its walks abroad to the horror and consternation of the former inmates.

On the ground floor the house is but one room wide, for the reason that half its width is taken up by a gateway leading to the stables and coach shed at the rear. The ground floor consists of a hall and kitchen. On the upper floor are four bedrooms, two of which are over the archway mentioned before and two over the hall and kitchen. Of these, the front room, that over the hall, was used as a sitting-room by the late occupants. The other three rooms were used as bedrooms, the occupant of the house and his wife sleeping in one, their two daughters in another, while the third was occupied by his two sons, the elder of whom is twenty-four years of age. The house in question has been built within the past four years, and the tenant, whose experiences are here set forth, went into the house between three and four months ago, and left it only last week, having gone to reside at a house only a few doors away on the other side of the street, for the convenience of being near the stable, which the late tenant of the house still rents.

The late occupant, who told me the story, is not the man to whom you would ascribe ability to concoct experiences such as are here related. He is not evidently of a highly nervous or excitable temperament, neither is he other than a highly respectable man, judged of good repute among his friends, and one whose word is treated with respect. As he told me the story and conducted me to the scenes in which the events were enacted, I was struck above all things else with the man's sincerity. He believed himself every word he told me – that was apparent.

What follows is the previous tenant's account of his time in the supposedly haunted property, having vacated the premises a week earlier. While his name isn't supplied in the original article, he is referred to as Mr J. Lathom in later correspondence:

It's only a few days since we left the house. I couldn't stand having the nerves of my family upset as they were continually while we were here, so I moved out, and very glad they are to be out of it.

Now what I'm going to tell you are just the plain facts. After we came into the house in the late autumn everything was quiet and proper for about a fortnight, and then one night my two sons, who were sleeping together, heard rapping in their room during the night. They said it appeared to be on their clothes box, which stood near the bed. When they told me I replied that it was all bosh, all humbug. After that the knockings were heard by other members of my family, but still I thought it was mere imagination, and that there was nothing in it. However, shortly afterwards, one evening when my wife and I had retired to our bedroom we heard two very loud and distinct raps on our bedroom door. I said to my wife that I supposed it must be one of the members of our family, and I got up quickly and opened the door, and to my astonishment saw nothing.

Very early one morning soon after, I believe it was about two o'clock, one of my daughters woke up suddenly and saw a shadow on the wall of her bedroom, and at the same time heard a curious noise. Her sister who was sleeping with her also woke up and remarked upon the noise, asking her what time it was, and said she supposed we hadn't all gone to bed as she could hear the chink of money as if I was counting up.

One night my wife distinctly heard the door of the front room, which she had left latched, open and shut again, and when we looked in the morning it was closed just as we had left it overnight. One evening last week, one of my daughters was in one of the upstairs rooms, about five o'clock in the evening, taking down a picture, when suddenly she felt a tug at her dress behind. She looked round, fancying it must have been a sister, but to her astonishment she saw no one.

Now, the last experience which occurred to myself is different from all the others. I was going down town, and before I went out I went upstairs. My wife asked me if I wanted a candle, and said 'no', I could find what I wanted without the aid of a light. As I was going up the stairs all of a sudden I had a most strange and extraordinary feeling, quite different to anything I had ever experienced in my life before. On a sudden my blood seemed to grow quite cold, to freeze within me, as if something had passed through me, and then after a moment I felt all right again. I seemed before it came on to have the sensation that something was coming down the stairs and was passing me, but though I looked and could see nothing. I never had such a feeling before.

But the former inhabitant's accounts didn't end there – there was even more activity outside of the property:

The most alarming ones have been outside. Of course, I have been for a long time past in the habit of going out late at night, between eleven and twelve o'clock to stable up the horses down at the bottom of the yard. Several times when I have been out there alone I have distinctly heard footsteps on the ceiling of the stable, as if someone were walking about in the loft, overhead. Several times when I have heard this I have immediately gone up the steps from the yard, for there is no other entrance to the loft, to see if anyone was about, but I have never seen anything there at all. I thought at first perhaps it might have been the dog, but that was impossible as two or three times when I have heard the noise he was asleep in his kennel.

Now, I must tell you of one of the most extraordinary occurrences of all. Last Boxing evening I had come in pretty late, and had sat down by the fire in the easy chair, my wife being near me. My elder son, who is twenty-four years of age, came in after me, and seeing me in the chair with my eyes closed thought I was asleep. He said to his mother, 'Father looks fairly tired out, I'll go out and see after the horses.' I heard him say this, and said, 'Yes, do, and I'll come out as well in a moment.' A few moments later I went out after him, and when I got as far as the stable door saw how frightened he looked. He was all of a tremble, and in his endeavours to strike a match had dropped nearly half the box full. I asked him what was the matter, and he then told me that after he had come out of the door and was walking down the yard to the stable, passing the shed, which was empty, he suddenly saw quite plainly and distinctly the face of a woman clothed in white, which stole silently along at the back of the shed. He watched it glide along until its came to the end of the shed abutting on the back of the house, and when it came to the wall it vanished.

My son was very much scared. He never fairly believed in ghosts before that, and now doesn't know what to make out of it.

That was the end of the family's personal experiences, but the reporter had also heard accounts from previous tenants:

I have heard since that strange tappings were heard, and that one night the lodger got up and came down, and went to the stable to see if anyone was about. I also heard that a woman died in the house, but can't be sure of it. I'm thoroughly interested in the matter now, and should like to get to the bottom of it. But as I said before, my family were all greatly scared by what they saw and heard, and are very glad they have moved.

Days after the accounts were published, the property's landlord was quick to reply, and – as is customary in cases where the owner stands to lose revenue if their properties become tarred as haunted – dismissed the entire story as 'humbug', pointing out to the reporter what he saw as a few problems with the tale:

The landlord of the house remarked that it was strange that Mr Lathom, after having such strange experiences as he alleged, should now have had erected premises adjoining those wherein the ghost is alleged to walk, and separated from the spirit's favourite promenade by nothing more than a brick wall, which is, to say the least of it, as easily penetrated by a disembodied spirit as a hoop of tissue paper is by a circus rider.

With the case as it stood seeming to be one man's word against another's, the reporter sought out another former tenant to interview, who sided with the landlord, saying that 'during the time he lived in the house now alleged to be haunted he never heard rappings or anything that would lead him to believe that the tenement possessed supernatural tenants'.

Again backing up the landlord's claim, a Mr Mark Veysey wrote to the newspaper to point out that 'having read the account of the ghost story in the papers, and being the previous tenant, I think it is a lot of rot, having been in the house and yard at all hours, and never heard or seen anything to indicate a ghost'.

Even so, the matter didn't end there.

As the newspaper pointed out, 'considerable interest continues to be manifested in the ghost story', and the mail kept arriving, this time from a former tenant named only 'One Who Heard' who corroborated the suggestion that the house was haunted:

In your paper a report was published from Mr Mark Veysey concerning the Cardiff ghost of Montgomery Street, saying it was all rot and that there was nothing there. I wish to contradict his statement. Some time ago I lodged in the same house, and one evening while sitting in the kitchen between nine and ten o'clock I heard footsteps, apparently of a man, walk through under the archway. I thought it was someone requiring a cab and at once went out to see, but could find no one. I closed the small door of the large ones and went back by the fireside. I had not been sitting down very long when I heard footsteps again quite plain walking back through the archway. I went to the front door of the house, but I saw no one, so I am convinced there was something mysterious there then, and that it cannot be superstition.

Following the landlord's accusations, Mr Lathom himself wrote to the newspaper to further assert his honesty, and pointed out that the property-owner might have an ulterior motive of his own:

In answer to the letters which appeared in your paper wherein the landlord of the house described the strange noises as humbug, I wish to state that I or my family are not in the habit of spreading untrue reports. Everything that I have stated is the truth. Ghosts have not been my invention. I never at any time believed in such nonsense as that, but I took the noises as a warning of sickness or death, as many other people do. I also wish to state that I never left the house owing to the noises; it was through the landlord trying to sell the premises. I had arranged about stables before Christmas. I did not want to have to turn out of the place and have nowhere to put my things. The landlord never mentioned selling the property when I took the house. Trusting I am not trespassing too long on your valuable space, but I should like the public to know the truth.

As an epilogue to the tale, a letter from 'G. C. W.' proposes a possible solution to the problem, and at the same time relates a similar tale of an unwanted ghostly presence in a Cardiff house which was solved when the occupier confronted the unwanted guest and simply asked them to stop:

> Materialists should have some difficulty in adequately accounting for the almost universal persistency of the belief in ghosts. Of late people to some extent have come to the conclusion that spirits never perplex town populations, but reserve their attentions for old world villages, where faith is more fully alive and critical investigation less to be feared. One of my friends says the reason ghosts do not haunt town houses is that modern men have grown more wicked than their fathers – too wicked for respectable morality-observing ghosts to have anything to do with.
>
> Be that as it may, the finding of a haunted house in town is a rare circumstance, consequently we all turned with intense interest to your reporter's mystery of Montgomery Street, the apparition of the backyard, and the passing through an unfortunate burgess of 'The woman in white.' The story however is not so baffling as might be desired. I know one better. Whether the intruders were mice or goblins, the affair is not less mysterious.
>
> A Cardiff ratepayer, hard-headed, in a good way of business, who is recognised by all who know him as a man who tells the truth, as a general thing, thus describes his experiences. He sleeps in a house alone in a well-known Cardiff street, and was for a considerable period troubled nightly with raps, taps, scrapings and other noises not at all dissimilar to those of the tenants in Montgomery Street. These increased until repose in that room became a matter of impossibility. So one night the burgess alluded to, after a long succession of sleepless hours, determined to bring matters to a crisis. He was not afraid of ghosts, but he wanted sleep. So he got up and proceeded to reason with the noises, or the producer of them. He pointed out that he had many things to do in this sphere, and wasn't prepared to go down below yet. 'All this,' he observed familiarly, like the frog in the fable, to the manifestor, 'all this may be fun to you, but it's death to me!' and ended the harangue by politely requesting his tormentor, 'angel from Heaven, or goblin damned,' to say what he wanted or leave!
>
> Now comes the remarkable part. From that moment not another sound was heard! As I said, whether the intruders were mice or ghosts, the thing is out of the common. If mice, they must have been of a very intelligent kind. I may add that this man believes in ghosts, and professes to have seen materialised forms, which have vanished, in full daylight, and open-air, and in the presence of three witnesses.

Terrifying nocturnal visits

Lisvane Church. (John Thorn)

In 1882, a poltergeist was said to be disturbing the residents of a cottage in the Cardiff village of Lisvane at night with sounds, damage, and even pulling the bedclothes from one person as they slept. A correspondent wrote that:

> Some of the inhabitants of the usually quiet little village of Lisvane are just now greatly disturbed by the nightly visitations of what they unitedly venture to call a ghost. About midway between the Parish Church and the Welsh Baptist Chapel is a small cottage occupied by a widow and her three or four children. There is also in the house a lodger, who has reached an advanced age.

And it was the lodger who had the most 'terrifying' nocturnal visits. One night he 'felt the bed clothes all carried away from him', and got up to strike a light. He 'searched in terror wild', but couldn't find the source of the disturbance:

> After having looked in vain under the bed, and carefully examined every hole and corner of the house, the lodger resolved to return to bed. He no sooner began to doze than the bedclothes were removed a second time. To his utter amazement he could see nothing, neither could he hear anybody in the house.

But he was not alone in being targeted, and the other occupants of the home also experienced strange happenings:

The widow and her children constantly hear chairs drawn about the house, and cups, saucers, and bottles crashing as if broken into a thousand pieces. The occupants of the little cottage have been terrified to such a degree that they dare not go into a dark room lest they should feel the ghost pulling at their clothes behind or its cold hands on their flesh.

It naturally caught the imagination of the villagers, and with so much interest in the 'mysterious proceedings which are nightly taking place at the cottage that the matter has been put before an eminent gentleman who is well versed in the doctrine of spiritualism, and whose reply they are now anxiously awaiting'.

6

THE GHOSTS OF INDUSTRY

Miners are possibly no more superstitious than other men of equal intelligence; I have heard some of their number repel indignantly the idea that they are superstitious at all; but this would simply be to raise them above the level of our common humanity.

Much like the new-fangled steam-powered locomotives which were hurtling around the once-peaceful countryside, industry advanced at an unprecedented rate during the Victorian era.

But while the onward march of progress had begun to dispel many of the long-standing myths and legends once so prevalent in Wales, there were new supernatural horrors for the 'superstitious folk' to fear following the Industrial Revolution.

Tales of ghosts soon found themselves attached to the modern ways of the world, where they lurked deep underground, prowled the railways, and prophesied impending doom for the workers who risked their lives on a daily basis. Many of these stories often had natural explanations, and for those working in such unforgiving conditions, a lone bat or a stray cat could be easily mistaken for a sinister entity. There were also those who artificially created hauntings as pranks or for ulterior motives, including one foreman who fabricated the illusion of a spirit in order to scare one of his workers into quitting his job – and the ploy worked.

The following article, published in 1894, looked at some of the superstitions which were said to prevail among Welsh miners:

Besides the association of the presence of the evil one with mines, there is a shadowy belief, scarcely reduced to a proposition, that the spirit of anyone killed in a pit hovers round the spot at any rate until after the body is consigned to sacred earth. To this idea is doubtless due the custom of suspending work in a pit when a fatal accident happens. All the men engaged in that part of the working come up out of the mine and do not descend the shaft until after the funeral.

Offering, as coalpits do, a sudden and irrevocable fate, as well as many chances of concealment, the disused shafts or old workings are often resorted to by those wretched creatures who feel life's burden too great to bear, and they have been taken advantage of to hide the horrid proofs of murder. It is not surprising, therefore, that when a pit has been made notorious by some such tragedy, it should be popularly supposed to be haunted, and be shunned accordingly. The gaunt, gallows-like structure which surmounts the shaft, the bare and bleak mount of pit spoil, and the weird lights that play on it from surrounding fires are sufficiently gloomy; but when to these is added the idea of a ghostly visitant, it is not to be wondered at that footpaths which lead across such a bank become neglected after dark.

But what of the incidents which can't be so easily dismissed as superstition?

The haunted ironworks

The following account recalls a 'remarkable adventure' which occurred at the Cyfarthfa Ironworks in 1881.

The article begins with the news editor dismissing the claims as the fancies of those who have had one drink too many, 'an hallucination occasioned by "spirits" emanating rather from the genial precincts of the "Castle" or the "Bush"'.

But the Merthyr correspondent who wrote the original story was keen to stress that it was 'vouched for on unimpeachable authority' and, despite his superior's scepticism, pointed out that no rational explanation had been offered for the unexplainable events as described below by a nameless witness:

> I had occasion to visit Cyfarthfa Works at night lately, and did so in company with a friend. What my business was must remain unexplained, enough that it was towards the gloomiest part of the night that we sallied forth, and made our way over tramroads and intricate paths to the scene. Cyfarthfa Works had been familiar to me for many years, but they were associated with the fullest activity, with the glare of furnaces, the whirl of the rolls; and that picture was vividly in my imagination when we stood at length before the works that were slumbering in thick darkness, and as silent as the grave.
>
> No change could have been greater, no stillness more profound. We were far enough from the town to lose its glare and its noise, and out of the way of the people journeying from one place to another. No place could thus be more isolated, even as no contrast from the wild dash of work to utter quietude could be more intense. We stood a while just within the dense shadow of one of the mills, just tracing the ponderous wheels and the dimly outlined rolls when suddenly the huge wheels creaked and began to revolve, the rolls to move, and in a moment there was all the whirl of industry again, only needing the glare of light and forms of men to assure us that the works were in full action. My companion, with an exclamation of profound astonishment, clasped me by the arm. Cool, iron man as he is, strong-minded and proof against the superstitions of the age, I felt his voice tremble, as he said, 'This is most strange. There are no men here; the works are stopped; no steam, no motive power.' And the grip on my arm became severe. I, too, felt alarmed, and am not ashamed to confess it. My imagination, livelier than that of his,

conjured up misty shades, and I saw shapes flitting to and fro, and heard the cry of men and boys amidst the clanging iron. Involuntarily we stepped back into the air, and as suddenly as the medley arose, so it died away; not a wheel moved, all was hushed, and at rest.

We walked away a little distance, our purpose unaccomplished, and talked to each other about this extraordinary incident. My friend, better able than I to afford a clue, was, like myself, utterly at sea, and could give no explanation. 'But,' said he, resolutely, 'it must be fathomed, and we will find it out.' With these words he hurried back again to the works. I followed, and in a few minutes again stood looking into the silent mill. There was the same strange hush, the same weird gloom that appeared palpable did we but attempt to grasp it; but no sound. 'Was it fancy?' said my friend with his cheerful laugh. He had scarcely spoken when the great wheel again revolved, and machinery here and there, to the right, to the left, ponderous wheels and rolls, all sprang into motion, and the din of work was perfect in its fullness. With this came the clanging of falling iron, the rattle of trams sounded strangely alike, and again the impression was strong that puddlers and moulders flitted by, and ghostly labour went on. This was sufficient for us. We hurriedly left the scene, and on our way home met one of the old ironworkers of Cyfarthfa going to Cefn, to whom my friend related the circumstance. He knew the man as an old and respectable inhabitant, and made no secret of what we had heard. 'Ha,' said the veteran, stopping and leaning on his stick, 'I have heard it too'; and, sinking his voice, he continued, 'it always comes when the works are stopped. It did one time before, many years ago, and when Mr Robert was living it came again. No one can say what is the reason, and perhaps it is best not to make any stir about it.'

The newspaper's cynical tone which preceded the report drew an 'indignant remonstrance' from one angry reader, who identified themselves as 'The Cyfarthfa Ghost'. And as a 'ghost', they offered their own thoughts on the matter, and pointed out one explanation which might connect the events to the former owners, the highly successful Crawshay family who had overseen the ironworks for nearly a century:

I resent indignantly the attempt of your correspondent to put such a commonplace interpretation on the cause of the mysterious events. If we can move a table, why not a wheel? If we can start musical boxes and send them playing around the room, why not wake up the music of machinery, rusty as it is? But no; if one of us should appear to a benighted yokel, it is put down as a turnip.

If Jones looks up at night, out of his sleep, just in time to behold a ghost flitting away, it is 'optical delusion,' or Williams hear sounds it is 'that pork sausage.'

This is always the way; but the explanation of an old woman at Cyfarthfa may be taken as very much nearer the truth. The good old soul lifted up her hands in astonishment when she heard of it, and then exclaimed, 'I believe it, every word. Bless your heart, the Crawshays loved their works as a father does his children, and they would not rest easy in their graves to see them stopped.' Good old woman.

The Pit of Ghosts

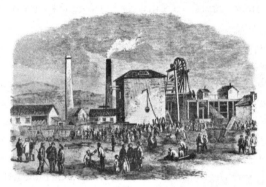

Morfa Colliery, Port Talbot, shortly after the 1863 explosion. (*Illustrated London News*, 1863)

Working in the mines was a perilous profession, and tragedy, it seemed, lurked around every corner.

One of the worst Welsh mining disasters to occur during the Victorian era was the Morfa Colliery disaster of 1890 where eighty-nine people lost their lives in an explosion, and saw the Port Talbot colliery become known as the 'The Pit of Ghosts'.

But it wasn't the first time that tragedy had struck the ill-fated coalmine. A series of explosions saw four men lose their lives in 1858, a further forty in 1863, and twenty-nine in 1870.

Any location surrounded by so much suffering would naturally find itself connected with ghost stories, but what was unique about the Morfa Colliery is that many of the ghost sightings occurred before – as well as after – the deaths of the workers. In fact, some of the earlier reports of activity, such as the oft-seen 'Ghost Dog of Morfa', were considered to be harbingers of impending doom, and there were some who refused to work in the colliery following the sightings – and lived to tell the tale as a result.

The press, on the whole, remained sceptical of claims that the workers had been warned by spectral messengers before the 1890 tragedy, and one cynical writer in the *Evening Standard* flatly dismissed such reports by boldly stating that 'collieries are too modern to be haunted. A haunted colliery is as ridiculous as a haunted railway station.'

Be that as it may, reports of strange occurrences in the coalmine continued, and what follows are accounts from those who were there at the scene, either working for the colliery or journalists investigating.

Our first report was published in 1890, two days after the disaster, and recalls some of the workers' fears just days before the catastrophe:

> Strange as it may appear, it is beyond a doubt that the belief has for a long time been entertained by the Morfa workmen that the pit was haunted. It has been said by reliable men that there were strange noises heard 'like thunder in a distance, and the slamming of air-doors' during the last week, and strange visions alleged to have been seen in the colliery. This was the talk of the neighbourhood previous to the sad occurrence, and was the subject of conversation among the workmen before going in on Monday morning, several hours before the disaster took place. It is further alleged two or three weeks ago several workmen left the pit because of these 'visions,' which they regarded as presentiments of coming evil, and went to work in the Maesteg and other valleys.

One survivor, Benjamin Nicholas, who was rescued following a 'ten-hour struggle' in the aftermath of the disaster, told the press that 'I have heard it said for some time now that it is haunted. Some say they have seen ghosts there, and that unearthly sounds and screams have been heard on several occasions. I have never heard nor seen anything myself, but I know several who say they have.'

A month later, an inquiry was under way to investigate the cause of the disaster, and with a thorough assessment on-going, the subject of ghosts naturally cropped up. The following report records how workers had asked for an inquiry into the strange sightings prior to the explosion:

> One singular incident was related in the course of the inquiry. Some short time before the explosion the men asked for a thorough inspection of the mine. Several of the witnesses were questioned as to the reasons for this

request. The answer was that the men thought there were spirits in the mine. Strange sounds had been heard, and it was believed that something would be seen at the bottom of the Cribbwr vein. In short, an impression prevailed that the mine was haunted, and that an inspection would put the spirits to flight. Perhaps further evidence is required before we can believe the story. The object of the questions was apparently to do away with the idea that the men had demanded an inspection because they were not convinced of the safety of the mine, and the witnesses may have been unconsciously influenced by a desire to give an explanation favourable to the management. It must be said, however, that one of those who spoke to the fear of ghosts was a working inspector nominated by the men. If superstition really enters into the case it may affect the thoroughness of an inspection. The inspector himself may hesitate to pry into bad and unfrequented corners.

For all these claims of unusual activity at the colliery, the press, on the whole, remained unconvinced that anything paranormal had or was occurring. One 'local gossip' column, which labelled the workers' claims as 'absurd', suggested a much more natural explanation:

> The absurd notion got abroad amongst some of the unfortunate colliers employed at the Morfa Colliery that it was haunted. These notions probably had their origin from the fact that the workings extend to the sea, and the rumbling noise is such as is frequently heard in underground workings when the sea is rough. One miner is said to have been so frightened by these noises that three weeks ago he refused to go underground and continued to the last firm in his refusal, saying that he heard similar noises when the explosion of 1870 occurred, and he had a presentiment that a like disaster could not be far off again.

The Fright of the Morfa Colliers

Nearly six years after the 1890 disaster at Morfa Colliery, the intrepid paranormal investigator known as 'Morien' decided to investigate the scene where 'strange noises' were still being heard.

What follows are extracts from her first-hand study entitled 'The Fright of the Morfa Colliers':

Morfa Colliery is about a mile and a half from the village of Taibach, which is on the sides of the high road between Margam Park and Aberavon. The way pedestrians reach the colliery is along a short railway from the Taibach Copperworks to the colliery. Tuesday afternoon was fine, but cloudy, and the moaning of the sea, a short distance away on the right, came from beyond the white mist of the lowering atmosphere. One heard, too, seawards, the seagulls whistling to their mates as if in search of each other in the fog. The 'moaning of the bar' and the pipings of the seabirds seemed like weird accompaniments to the alleged supernatural cries heard many fathoms deep in the underground workings of the colliery, whose tall engine-gear loomed in the distance through the white mist before one as he walked rapidly in their direction.

At Taibach I found the Morfa colliers standing in groups at the street corners. Being descendants of the ancient Silurians, these men are very brave, and, like their ancestors, they would meet a charge of cavalry on foot. But, if they are equal to all kinds of flesh and bones either in war or peace, they are terribly afraid of ghosts! It is all very well for the reader, seated in the daylight at his fireside, to call the Morfa colliers 'superstitious,' because they on hearing strange and unexplainable noises in the dark caverns of the earth, hundreds of yards below where the swans ride the waters, turn tail and bolt towards the light of the sun.

One of the colliers today, standing among his fellows, with his hands in his pockets, a pipe in his mouth, told me he had read the editorial comments in the 'Western Mail' that morning on what they were pleased to call the 'superstition' of the Morfa colliers. 'Tell the editor,' he said, severely, 'to confine his remarks to things of this world, for he knows nothing about heaven and hell and the workings underground!' And he added the remark that if the editor had been seated in the dim light of a Clanny lamp in the interior of the workings, and had heard groaning in the darkness beyond and below in the deep, he, too, would have taken to his heels, and quickly sought 'some hole or another to hide in.'

Another collier, sharp-eyed and seemingly highly intelligent, declared to me, there was not the slightest doubt that inexplicable strange noises had been heard in the workings both lately and before the explosion six years ago. This belief, which he declared ninety per cent of the men believed, has been intensified by the finding of the dove at ten o'clock on Sunday night close to the mouth of the shaft. Lowering his voice, and his face the picture of solemnity, the same young man said to me as follows:– 'In the Bible the dove has a unique position. The Church is there alluded to as a cooing dove in the wilderness. The Holy Spirit assumed the shape of a dove in its descent upon the head of our Lord at His baptism. It was a dove that was sent out of Noah's ark in search of daylight after the deluge, and,' added he, 'how do we know but that the dove perched in the night on that tram, close to the weigh-house, and near the pit's mouth, might not be a signal warning us of our peril?'

On reaching the pit's mouth I ascertained that Mr Robson, the Government inspector; Mr Grey, the chief manager; Mr Isaac Evans, miners' agent; and eight of the men had gone down into the mine in search of the 'spirits,' if any were really there. It struck me there was something peculiar in the numbers gone down to exorcise the 'spirits'. Mr Robson, Mr Grey, and Mr Isaac Evans seemed to be engaged after the manner of the Egyptian trimurti. The eight workmen represented the seven planets and the Ogdoad or Octave. When I ascertained the order with which they had gone to face the 'enemy', I instantly concluded that he would take care to make himself scarce on the occasion of their visit. On their return to bank, after spending several hours below, they declared they had neither seen nor heard anything. Mr Grey however, looked very serious. Probably, his seriousness on this occasion was mainly attributable, not to the ghost or ghosts, but to the annoyance he felt at the stoppage of the colliery through the men declining to go down. It was understood the men still refused to resume work. But immediately after ascending out of the pit Mr Isaac Evans and the eight men representing the other underground workmen returned to Taibach to report the result of the exploration. The full body of workmen would then come to some final agreement as to whether work should be resumed or not today.

The story of the fright is briefly as follows:– A short time before the explosion six years ago several workmen declared they had heard strange noises in the workings. It is stated that several men were so frightened by what they had heard that they left of their own accord and went to work in the Rhondda Valley. Among other things then said was that an apparition, dressed in a black oilcloth suit, had ascended from the shaft by the side of a tram of coal on the cage, and that it had been seen walking across the yard to the place used as a deadhouse after the explosion. One of the officials of the colliery, dressed exactly in the same manner, did as the apparition had done immediately after the disaster had happened. On the present occasion, in addition to finding the dove as stated on Sunday night, two men declared they heard a few days ago groans issuing from a part of the workings unoccupied. In addition to this, it is stated a heavy door on one of the roadways was seen to open and shut of its own accord, and a canvas door was seen fluttering in a most mysterious fashion.

The entire locality is much moved in reference to the affair, and among other things, as indicating the possibility of things supernatural appearing, refer to the witch of Endor raising by the request of King Saul the ghost of the prophet Samuel. It must be admitted that it seemed that a small minority laughed merrily over the tales told.

Blood-curdling ghosts of the mines

When 'Morien' decided to revisit the scene of the Morfa Colliery disaster, it reignited interest with the supernatural incidents surrounding the tragedy not only amongst the public, but also in the journalist who had originally reported from the scene of the explosion.

In a new article published in December 1895, he explained that some of the more 'blood-curdling' aspects of the case had been omitted from his original report, but now that others were digging deeper into the incidents, he felt more inclined to reveal them. And not only about Morfa, but also accounts from other Welsh mines as well.

'Some of the cases which I have come across are of a far more blood-curdling character than any yet published in connection with the present scare,' he said in his introduction, before giving an example of a recent sighting of a spectral lady at the Albion Colliery in Cilfynydd:

Only a few months ago some of the miners declared in awe-struck whispers that in a certain portion of that colliery might be seen any night the figure of a woman looking for her husband, who had been killed in the terrible explosion at that colliery many months before. The strange part of it was the woman, whose name was given, had died shortly after the Albion catastrophe, and, as she had made nightly visits to the colliery yard before her death, it was gravely asserted by those people that her spirit still haunted portions of the mine in continuation of the quest which she had so steadfastly pursed when in the body. I do not know that any explanation of this story came out, and, of course, the colliery was not stopped on account of it, and the rumour died out. But I give the anecdote in order to illustrate the statement that colliery ghosts are by no means scarce even in these days.

Turning his attention back to Morfa, he noted that the details he was about to disclose were all 'the result of interviews which I had with workmen whose lives had been saved at Morfa, and I have not the slightest doubt that the men considered they were telling the truth'. These included some of the already-mentioned sightings reported elsewhere, but which were missing some key facts:

> The man dressed in oilskins was one of a series of extraordinary visions which these people professed to have come across. He was stated to have jumped the cage and travelled upward with a cageful of men, although he only joined them after the cage had started (suddenly appearing amongst them like a ghost, of course), and then dismounted at the lower landing, although the cage did not stop there. But, then, there came the vision of the 'red dog,' which travelled underground, and which nobody knew anything about. The noises also were then present, and the most extraordinary part to me of the whole account was the statement that all of a sudden an overpowering smell of roses was noticed by some – similar to the odour in a room where a body was lying in state, and when the wreaths and crosses of flowers surrounded it – and I was gravely told that this odour pervaded portions of the workings of the Morfa Colliery.

Following the publication of his initial report in 1890, the reporter says that he was visited at home by a 'respectable miner, who now lives in the lower part of the Rhondda Valley'. While no name is given, he is described as having 'strong religious beliefs, and occupies, I believe, the position of Sunday School superintendent'. The miner cautiously inquired as to whether the newsperson believed all that he had written on the subject, and confident that he was speaking with someone who would take reports of strange phenomena seriously, he related the following events, both of which involve leg-breaking incidents:

> Receiving an assurance from me that I felt certain that those who told me the stories believed in them, he proceeded to express his own implicit belief in the statements. He had, he said, received ample proof in his own person of the truth of such stories of underground visions. He, whilst working at the Great Western Colliery at Ynysybwl and at Penygraig, had experienced what he termed the value of supernatural signs underground. Now, as the instances

are somewhat personal, I refrain from mentioning at which of the collieries the various incidents happened, but I will 'lump' them.

In one case, he said, he and his 'partner' went into their working place, and before they had done a stroke of work he noticed that the place was filled with a brilliant light, which he took to be a sign from another world. He turned to his partner, and said it was not safe for them to remain there and work. His partner asked him what made him think so, and my informant solemnly asked his partner whether he did not see the light, to which his partner replied that he saw nothing. When my informant told me this I remarked it was an extraordinary thing that his partner could not see it if it was there, and his reply was that it was 'not given to his partner to see it.' He decided to leave the place and go home, because he believed that the light was a sign to him that something was going to happen, but his partner remained where he was. On the way out my friend met one of the minor officials of the colliery, who swore at him for leaving his work, and laughed at his tale of 'a vision of light.' That official, he told me, sent his own son to fill the place, and, in less than two hours after that son had been at work, a fall came down and broke the young man's leg, thus verifying the ground of the fear which had made the man himself go out, yet, strange to say, his partner, who had not seen the light, escaped unhurt.

In order to show me the perils of unbelief, the man gave me another instance of a 'sign' given him. In that case it was not a light, but a voice, calling him by name in a warning tone. I asked him what the voice said, and he replied, 'Nothing except my name.' On that occasion, he said, he debated the matter with himself, and decided to remain where he was, believing that he had only imagined hearing the voice. But he had only worked half his turn before his leg was broken by a stone which fell from the top.

Finally, the correspondent relates a story told to him by Mr Lewis Williams, a mining engineer from Upper Boat in Pontypridd, who is described as 'a gentleman who would not be regarded by those who know him as very likely to be imbued with superstitious fears, yet what he heard made each particular hair on his head stand on end "like quills upon the fretful porcupine".'

In this case, a rational – and more importantly, life-saving – explanation was found, but it still serves as a good illustration of how the ideas of a haunted mine could play tricks on the workers' minds:

Lest it may be said that my leg-breaking ghosts are too gruesome, allow me to vary the programme by giving another illustration of a colliery official who was frightened almost out of his wits by a ghostly voice. He occupied the post of a colliery manager for a company further 'down the west' than the Morfa, and at times, was rather anxious about the safety of the pit, owing to the bursting of occasional blowers of some magnitude. One weekend he had to go away from home, and when he returned on Sunday morning he felt uneasy, and decided to descend the pit alone. He got the engineman to let him down the shaft, and went over a portion of the workings without finding anything wrong. He was returning towards the pit bottom when, all of a sudden, he fancied he heard a scream. He stopped, and, after a few seconds, heard another scream, like that of a young girl. His indignation, as a father, was instantly aroused as he thought of the possibility of a child having been hidden in that lonely mine, and he instantly retraced his steps in the direction of the sound. Every now and then that scream would be repeated, and, as he got nearer, it became more shrill. Then it would die out with a moan, and afterwards there was dead silence. The girl had evidently fainted. He walked and walked but to no purpose, and was almost giving up in despair, when he heard a terrific scream between him and the pit bottom. Knowing that no human being could have escaped his vigilant search, he began to be imbued with sinister thoughts, and wondered whether he had not been somewhat rash to risk his life in going into the pit alone. He kept repeating to himself, 'Well, I don't believe in ghosts, but I shall have a chance of seeing one if it is here.' He stood to cogitate, when, within a few feet of him, there arose a shrill scream which lasted a few seconds, and terrified him almost out of his wits, and then there was a whistling sound which sounded like a 'blower' of gas. He walked back very slowly, and then found gas oozing from a fissure in a rock right under his feet, the pressure of 'the squeeze,' as colliers call it, causing it to whistle like a railway steam engine, and when the pressure was eased the sound ceased, thus accounting for the variations of silence and ghostly 'noise.' He thus solved his own ghost story, and was enabled to get the mine cleaned of an accumulation of gas, which might next day have sent every soul in that colliery into eternity.

A Christmastime caution

In our final round-up of accounts associated with Morfa Colliery, a 'weird story' emerged just after Christmas 1895 when hundreds of employees downed their tools and refused to work following 'strange activity'. It was reported that:

for some days past work has been suspended, and three hundred colliers have been kicking their heels on the surface. On Friday morning the men went down again, their nerves in a high state of tension and their families and neighbours wound up to a great state of excitement. What was it all about? It appears that a few days ago strange and uncanny sounds were heard by some of the miners. Two men were sitting side by side 'ar dro'r heol' (at the turn in the road); beyond were miles of old workings shrouded in darkness. Suddenly out of the void came a succession of piercing wails, horrible to hear. The pitmen did not stay to clear up the mystery, but took to their heels, spreading the alarm as they went.

The report spread that some influence of an unhallowed and ominous kind was busy in the workings, and the men elected to stay above ground until a thorough examination had been made. Their fears were confirmed by a fresh omen. In the early hours of Sunday morning a dove was found at the pit's mouth. Opinions differed as to the exact significance of the portent. That it is a ghostly messenger is widely held. This particular dove was not white enough to be above suspicion or dark enough to make its nether origin certain.

While reports of this nature were hardly uncommon at Morfa, what is interesting about this case is that the activity was also witnessed by somebody unconnected with the coalmine itself, and the timing coincided with what the miners had experienced on site:

The mystery became deeper the more the theologians and experienced people discussed it. But testimony came in due time confirming the story of the men who heard the cries. A gamekeeper on the hills near Hafod Farm heard the sound of the singing of dirges come straight up the glen from the direction of the Cross, which is the name of the Calvinistic Methodist Chapel between Margam Abbey and Taibach. Were the monks of Margam chanting in their shrouds to keep the ghosts of the Methodists at arm's length? The gamekeeper is not clear on that point. But the dirges were heard at four in the morning, the very hour when the wild cries swept through the pit workings below. About the same time, too, a door was seen to open and shut of itself in one of the galleries of the mine. The managers of the mine seem to have behaved very sensibly. They asked the Government Inspector to make a full investigation of the workings, and this official, in company with the men's agent and a small party, spent several hours below on Thursday, and came up with a most reassuring report. And on the strength of this the men threw aside their fears and went down again as usual.

Finally, in an update published in 1896, ghostly events had once again returned to Morfa, and for the first time a number was put on the amount of ghosts thought to haunt the coalmine, an explanation to their identities, and the activity associated with them:

> Morfa Colliery has been infested with restless spirits for about a week. They are supposed to be six in number, and to be the ghosts of some miners who were killed in an explosion. They make their presence known by wailing and knocking all over the underground workings. These diversions, it is said, they vary by the singing of dirges and the roll of muffled drums.

The ghost train from the future

For those living in the remote rural areas of Wales, some of which had remained essentially unchanged for generations, the arrival of the rail tracks which spread like a spider's web across the land in the nineteenth century brought with it a natural sense of apprehension.

In one unusual case from 1864, a farmer from Carmarthenshire was given the fright of his life by one of these new bone-shaking forms of transport – but before it had actually arrived.

Describing the apparition as a 'ghost train from the future', the reporter covering the story believed that some form of clairvoyance might have been in action, noting that 'the Welsh are said to be endowed with the power of prophecy, or "second sight"'.

What follows is an account of the evening's proceedings:

> A farmer and his friend had been enjoying a day's fishing in the Tav, an excellent trouting stream that runs past the old Abbey of Whitland. As evening drew on the sport grew slack, and at last the trout gave up taking at all, so the sportsmen put up their tackle, said 'Good night,' and departed on their several roads homeward.
>
> The farmer, however, liked a pipe, and was stopping with the intention of lighting his, when he became conscious of an indescribable sensation; the

air seemed full of sound, and yet was perfectly silent. As he stood perplexed, not to say alarmed, strange noises began to issue from the ground, the hill trembled beneath his feet, his pipe dropped from his hand, and he was on the point of running away, when a long whistling shriek, accompanied by the sound of a thousand wheels, burst from the hillside close behind him; a number of horses feeding close by pricked up their ears and galloped wildly down the hill, jumping right into the bed of the Tav, where they stood panting and frightened until the strange sound died away in the distance.

The farmer did not stay to pick up his pipe, but hurried home brim-full of the wonderful event, and under considerable apprehension that some terrible calamity was going to happen to him or his family. Sometime afterwards the line for the South Wales Railway was surveyed and a tunnel at last completed, the mouth of which opened at the very spot from whence as was now explained a spectral train had issued, and upon the opening day the farmer and a crowd of country folk were upon the spot to witness the effect, which certainly exactly answered the description given by him, even to the horses galloping into the Tav.

7

SACRED GROUND AND SUPERSTITION

Who is there that has never felt an instinctive awe as he passed along at midnight through a lonely churchyard in a deserted village, as the white moon shimmered on the half-hidden gravestones?

Old beliefs die hard, as they say, and some of the accounts from the Victorian era remained firmly rooted in the folklore stories of days gone by. Sightings of corpse candles and phantom funerals persisted in some areas, and as one correspondent in 1864 noted – some might say unfairly – 'as a people, the Welsh are much given to superstition'.

Be that as it may, the people were also deeply religious and, unsurprisingly, a lot of the ghostly sightings centred on holy sites such as the local churches, chapels, abbeys and, possibly most popular of all, the graveyards.

The Church itself, the great bastion of morality in Wales, seemed to have formed an uneasy alliance with the secular nature of popular science at the time. But while opinions within the clergy remained divided on such ground-breaking advances as the theory of evolution, it appeared to be totally unprepared for the rise in popularity of spiritualism.

Such distractions as table tipping and communicating with the dead through séances were originally seen by many as harmless parlour games. But the spiritualists were soon posing some very difficult questions on the very nature of the human soul, and seemed to be offering more answers about the spirit world than Christianity itself. The men of the cloth reacted in different ways, with some sternly renouncing it as the work of the Devil, others embracing it as further proof of a Christian afterlife, while there were those who kept their heads down and hoped the whole thing would just evaporate into thin air like the phantoms themselves.

Wherever these spirits were coming from – heaven, hell, purgatory, or the fervent imagination of the 'superstitious' people – they remained ingrained in the minds, and in the holy places, of Wales.

The mysterious white mist

Under the right conditions, naturally forming white mist can, unsurprisingly, appear eerie and paranormal, and continues to be mistaken for something more otherworldly to this day.

But in this account from the vicinity of a churchyard in 'the wild mountains of North Wales' in 1901, not only did the observers see the white mist but, believing it to be supernatural in nature, they attempted to uncover its true purpose – and were left convinced that what they had encountered was not of this earth:

The inhabitants of a small village, not twenty miles from Wrexham, were startled by the appearance of a ghost. A few of the villagers were chatting together at about 10.30pm (an early hour for the old-fashioned ghosts), when one of them noticed a being, apparently intent on joining the party. A shapeless mass of white had silently and mysteriously loomed up in the darkness not ten yards from them, and seemed to be approaching from the direction of the churchyard.

It was at first supposed to be the work of a practical joker, but a suggestion to pelt it with stones (a sure test in such cases) had no effect. One of the nobler members of the party took his life in his hand and approached the thing. It swiftly evaded his grasp and glided silently towards the churchyard. After going a few yards it gave forth some inarticulate sounds and mysteriously disappeared, returning, we suppose, to its infernal regions.

Some scoffers have ridiculed the possibility of ghosts, but we are sure that none of those who saw the weird thing, about five foot six inches in height, the head going up to a point, apparently without arms or legs, will ever forget the sight, or for a moment doubt its supernatural nature.

The funeral procession of spirits

Llanychllwydog Church and graveyard, which has since been
converted into a private house. (Ceridwen)

In an article published in 1898, it was noted that in Wales it was 'very seldom that death took place without some spirit appearing beforehand to signify to the neighbours, if not to the household, that the doom of a friend was about to be settled'.

These precursors of death were said to appear in many guises, and would 'visit the neighbourhood in brilliant light, pacing the road from residence to graveyard. At other times a funeral procession was observed marching in regular order.'

Those who caught a glimpse of these premonitions could expect some bad news soon, that the end was near either for themselves, or for those in the coffin or their relations in the parade if they could identify them.

The following account of an event, which is said to have taken place some fifty years beforehand, relates to one such resident who encountered a spirit procession in Pembrokeshire and who, despite his probable intoxication at the time, could still be classed as a reliable witness:

About four miles from Fishguard, in a narrow valley called Cwm Gwaun, is an old church with a large burial ground, with a footpath through the middle. Although it was in those days a haunted place, people would take the footpath in preference to the road. The spirits of the dead lying in that consecrated ground seem to claim the graveyard as their abode.

Harri was generally under the influence of Sir John before he began his homeward journey, and therefore his courage was equal to his needs at any time. On this particular night, when he entered the path in the churchyard of Llanychllwydog, he observed a funeral procession marching in through the gateway at the other end. His valiant heart broke down at the sight, and he took his seat on one of the tombstones, not knowing whether or not he had sunk into the nether world. But he looked around, and Sir John's influence began to forsake him, and reason seemed to assume her throne, and Harri at the restoration of his reasoning faculties recognised his neighbours. Even the horses and carriages were objects he had no difficulty in knowing. Harri could name the persons and describe the order of the procession, and the words and intonations of the officiating priests were quite familiar to him for many a day after the solemn visions of that particular night.

The vision made a sober man of Harri'r Cwman for a long time. He could find his way from Fishguard to Cwman without alcoholic guidance. What is marvellous in this affair is that it turned out to be a fact. The person whose coffin appeared in an apparition was in a short time carried to the very grave where Harri had seen it laid, and the persons forming the procession appeared in the funeral as foreseen by the farmer of Cwm Gwaun.

The author stresses that he knew Harri'r Cwman well, and that while 'it is very true that he was under the influence of alcohol when the vision appeared, it is true also that he related the circumstances before they actually occurred'.

He adds that the place and circumstances surrounding the event are 'well known to the aged inhabitants of Cwm Gwaun, and the truth can be verified'.

Violent retribution

The following 'strange ghost story' was recorded in the Swansea Valley in 1878, and it tells of a man who, feeling wronged after his death, returns in spirit-form to violently accost his former acquaintances.

In life, he was part of a 'friendly society' in Pontardawe, and as a rule they would pay the funeral allowance for their members. But there was a condition – they would not pay the allowance in the case of a suicide, a crime which this former member was charged with committing.

According to the report, 'one of the members recently died by his own hand, and the club accordingly refused to pay the death money'. But following this 'just refusal', the remaining members began 'complaining that they are subjected to serious persecution from an unseen and, presumably, a ghostly agent'. The attacks began on a Sunday, when:

> one of the officers, returning home over a lonely road, was assailed by the spirit of the late member, who, failing to get a satisfactory reply to his demand for the money, in a somewhat unspiritlike manner assailed the unfortunate man, and actually 'tore his clothes to ribbons.' Such, at least, was the account he gave, in tones of horror, at the first public house he came to after this terrific encounter.

The next incident occurred on the following Tuesday evening:

> Whilst the members were assembled in the lodge-room, the usual knocks were heard at the door as of a brother seeking admittance. The door was opened, but no one was to be seen. The members, however, are all very certain that they heard the voice of the deceased utter the words 'Pay my widow my funeral money, and then I shall be at rest.' The meeting precipitately broke up, and the members are now puzzled to know what to do with such a determined deceased brother.

Sadly the trail ends here, and whether or not the ghost received his burial fee remains unknown.

The mysteries of the corpse candles

Of all the ghostly phenomena recorded in this book, possibly the most uniquely Welsh are the corpse candles, or *canwyll corff*.

The ghostly lights, which are interpreted as a sign of impending death, were explained by 'The Dutchman' in one of his regular compilations of 'Ghosts and Ghost Stories' from 1885. He quoted a Mr Davis for his description, whose account was derived from an article originally written in 1656 under the name Reverend John Davis of Generglyn in Richard Baxter's *Certainty of the World of Spirits* (1691).

It was noted that while corpse candles were common throughout Wales, they were particularly prevalent in 'the counties of Cardigan, Carmarthen, and Pembroke', and that 'they are called candles from their resemblance, not to the body of the candles but the fire'.

The candles are said to travel on a fixed route, possibly the same path a sick or a dying person will follow on the way to their upcoming funeral, and will change in appearance if they come within close proximity of a human being: 'In their journey, these candles are sometimes visible and sometimes disappear, especially if anyone comes near to them, or in the way to meet them. On these occasions they vanish, but presently appear again behind the observer, and hold on their course.'

The colours, quantities and direction of the corpse candles can also affect their meaning:

> If a little candle is seen, of a pale bluish colour, then follows the corpse, either of an abortive, or some infant; if a larger one, then the corpse of someone come to age. If there be seen two, three, or more, of different ages, some big, some small, then shall so many corpses pass together of such ages or degrees. If two candles come from different places, and be seen to meet, the corpses will do the same; and if any of these candles turn aside, through some bypath, leading to the church, the following corpse will be found to take exactly the same way. Sometimes these candles point out the places where persons shall sicken and die. They have also predicted the drowning of persons passing a ford.

He also describes a variation of the corpse candle, the tan-we or tan-wed, which is 'another kind of fiery apparition peculiar to Wales':

> This appeareth, to our seeming, in the lower region of the air, straight and long, not much unlike a flame. It moves and shoots directly and level, but far more slowly than falling stars. It lighteneth all the air and ground where it passeth, lasteth three or four miles or more, for aught is known, because no man seeth the rising or the beginning of it, and when it falls to the ground it sparkleth and lighteth all about. These commonly announce the death or decease of freeholders by falling on their lands, be he but a lord of a house and garden, but you shall find someone at his burial that hath seen this fire fall on some part of his lands.

It is said that they are seen by the very people whose deaths are foretold, and the narrator claims that there had been two such instances in his own family.

The Welsh Jack-o'-lantern

Reports of an 'extraordinary moving light' near Pontypridd made the headlines in 1898, causing 'considerable alarm' among those who believed that a corpse candle was prophesying a death in Llantwit Fardre.

It was spotted near the old Stank Pit by a local man who occupied a 'responsible position', and who solemnly declared that on two nights in succession he saw the 'dreaded ghost', which was thought to be a Jack y Lantern, the Welsh Jack-o'-lantern.

The reporter, who draws parallels with sightings of such 'fables' as Will o' the Wisp and *Bendith y Mamau* (Blessing of the Mothers, another name for the *Tylwyth Teg*, Welsh fairy folk), assures us that 'the story is told in all sincerity, and we are convinced that the spectator of the ghostly sight actually saw what he declares he witnessed in that lonely spot when the shades of night had fallen upon the landscape'.

Carrying a lighted lantern, the witness was walking through the old Stank Pit towards Church Village when 'he happened to gaze into the trees and bushes which grow thickly on each side of the road, and he fancied he saw a light in the midst of the trees'.

Assuming it was another person also carrying a lantern, he paused to see if his fellow traveller would be walking in the same direction, but they came no closer:

> Beyond moving up and down, and a little way backward and forward, there was no sign of advancing towards the road on the part of the extraordinary carrier of the peculiar light. The gentleman shouted to the man in the wood, but the only response, in the stillness of the night, was the echo of his own voice in the valley below. 'Hallo, there,' he cried, and 'Hallo, there,' came the answering echo from the surrounding trees, and 'Hallo, there,' came reverberating from the heights of the Garth and the slopes of the Bryn.
>
> He felt inclined to go to the rescue of the possible wayfarer who had lost his way in the wood, but he had an appointment to keep, or he would have explored the mystery. 'Hallo, there!' he again shouted, before starting off, but the silent light only flickered and played, and answered not! It remained there when he left, and, as he glanced backwards, he noticed the dancing light casting a lurid glare upon the overhanging boughs, and seemingly hovering on the brink of the old pit, or directing attention to where the stake of the martyr once stood when the fatal flame of religious persecution sent St Illtyd from earth to heaven in a chariot of living fire.

Believing that he had encountered a corpse candle, the man decided to make haste on his way to Church Village, where he stopped at the post office to tell Mr Bryant the postmaster of the 'queer vision' en route:

> Mr Bryant, and the Pontypridd postman, who happened to be there at the time, cheered him up by telling him some blood-curdling anecdotes of previous ghostly visitations at the Stank, and suggested that the light might possibly be that of the wandering spirit of someone who had fallen, or who had jumped, into the old pit. But the witness of the light was no coward, and though he declined to discuss the matter lightly, he promised to try to fathom the mystery, if possible, on the following night.

True to his world he did just that, and in order to dismiss the theory that what he'd seen was just 'the reflection of the light of his own lantern', he extinguished his own light just before arriving at the haunted spot:

The result was just what he had expected. In the midst of the bushy under-growth of the Stank Avenue, he observed, once more, the faint glimmer of the magic light of Jack y Lantern – the dread prowler of the Welsh marshes, whose flickering, gassy beacon often lured the unwary travellers of past gen-erations through bogs and dykes and ditches into the midst of hobgoblins, to be frightened into fairy rings to dance for a year and a day, or into the presence of the black being whose cloven hoofs, forked tail, and horned skull proclaimed him to be the Prince of the Kingdom of Darkness! It was there – at Llantwit! There could be no mistake about it, and, remembering the sad tale of a servant of his father who had once been led a pretty dance by the self-same Jack y Lantern, he positively declined to follow the dancing phantom light which seemed to beckon him to follow it off the high road, and when he reached the end of his journey he told, with bated breath, the extraordinary tale which has once more set Llantwit Fardre people recount-ing the legends of their childhood's days, and hunting up lost records of the previous visits to that neighbourhood of the sparkling sprite known as the Stank Ghost!

Revenge from beyond the grave

In 1886, John Humphreys from Caernarfon – the author of the ill-fated Berllan investigation covered in the 'Victorian Ghost Hunters' chapter – recalled a story of revenge from beyond the grave by an aggrieved mother whose family had seemingly ignored her final wishes.

The tale was told to him by a local woman, aged nearly 100 years old. She had grown up in a time when 'the good folk living in and about Caernarfon were densely, intensely, and ignorantly superstitious and belief in ghosts and their supernatural appearance was an unexceptional rule'. As such, 'a belief in such a story as I am about to relate would be the most natural thing in the world, and I, for one, am not surprised that my informant implicitly believes in its truth at the present day'.

Despite this, he does not commit to believing in the story himself, and decides to stick solely to presenting the facts as they were told to him. Also, the original author used various spellings for the name Jinney in this story, and occasionally changed it to Jenny. The following excerpts remain con-sistent with the most commonly used spelling of the name:

In the year 1810, John Jones and his wife, Jinney, lived in a substantial farm-house near Caeathro. They were comparatively well to do, and had an only daughter, named, after her mother, Jinney. At the time this story opens, Jinney's mother had just died, and her body lay in a room in the oil farm, awaiting interment. Her grave may now be seen at Llanbeblig.

Near Mr Jones' farm stood the 'big house' of Rhys Rhys, whose eldest son, an enigmatical sort of person, morose and taciturn, had fallen in love with Jinney Jones, and had obtained Mr Jones' consent to a marriage. Mrs Jones, however, disliked the idea of a match between her pretty daughter and the sour heir of the adjoining estate, and she had, up to her death, steadfastly refused to withdraw her opposition, and in this frame of mind had died, denouncing maledictions on the union if it were consummated after her death. As for Jinney herself, she appears to have been of an aspiring if somewhat flighty character, and, as far as she dared, ignored her mother's injunctions against keeping young Rhys' company. Many a sweet kiss was indulged in during the frequent lonely walks of the young couple around the lanes of what is now called Glan Gwna and Caeathro, and they vowed that come what might, as soon as propriety would admit after her mother's interment they would be married.

The day of the funeral arrived, wet, and gloomy with fog, and what was regarded as a supernatural darkness prevailed during the procession to Llanbeblig. The horrified mourners were also startled at intervals by the appa-rition of the deceased lady, which appeared frequently during the march to the church, gleaming spectrally among the trees on the roadside, and in such a form as impressed them with the conviction that the wraith was denouncing doom on those who had so secretly determined to ignore her dying wishes.

But the interment itself past off quietly, and all returned home, drenched to the skin by the sleet which fell all the morning, changing in the afternoon to a heavy fall of snow, which covered the whole countryside with a vast white mantle.

In Mr Jones' homestead only three persons remained, and one of them sat alone in the kitchen. In a smaller room, where a great wood fire burned, Jinney and Rhys sat together conversing in low tones on the events of the day, Rhys encouraging Jinney in her decision to marry him as soon as decency would permit.

The night closed, and Mr Jones pressed Rhys to stay rather than face mid-night terrors on his homeward journey. This the lover consented to do, and a new subject of conversation was started in the ghostly appearances of Mrs Jones during the funeral procession. But while they conversed, they became aware of a presence in the room, and their hearts almost stopped from fear. There was nothing to be seen; not a sound broke the deathly stillness of the night; yet they felt that, somewhere near them, all about them, an antagonistic supernatural influence prevailed, and choked their utterance. The fire waned and died; the watchers sat still in their places, staring dreadfully into the gloom; clutching each other's hands in an agony of terror. Every moment they expected some horrible vision to manifest itself; every moment they expected some ghastly outbreak of noise to affright their ears; but neither sound nor vision had they.

The long hours of the night passed, and the day broke, and the three watchers, hand-in-hand, woke from their trance with a shuddering cry of relief, and separated.

Three months passed, and Jinney Jones became Mrs Rhys. A large wedding party gathered in the Rhys Mansion, and dance and song rang through the old house. About eleven o'clock the party broke up, old John Jones being the last to leave. Rhys and his wife went with him to his lonely house, and bade him good night on the door steps. They then slowly traced their steps homeward. Arrived there, Jinney turned round to give a last glance at her old home, and immediately fell screaming to the ground. Rhys, who had turned to open the door, swung round to ascertain the cause of his bride's sudden terror.

To his unspeakable horror, on the sill of his father-in-law's bedroom window, burned the dim flame of the corpse candle, while all about him in the night air the deadly fear of the funeral night began to assert itself. Gradually the presence became manifest. Dimly outlined on the door of his house stood the wraith of Jinney's mother, menacing but silent. Rhys stood paralysed with fear. Not a movement could he make, either to pass into the house or to assist his bride. The eyes of the apparition regarded him with terrible persistence, but there was no voice or sound. And so the time passed – in reality but a few minutes, it seemed to Rhys endless.

The spell was for a moment broken by the recovery of his wife from the swoon into which she had fallen. Rhys stooped to raise her. But the moment she turned her eyes to the hall door, a more terrible cry than before rang through the night, and she dropped lifeless to the ground.

Lights now appeared, and servants ran up on all sides. Rhys regarded them wildly for a moment, then threw up his arms and fell heavily beside his dead wife. When they carried the bodies into the house, life had passed from the bride. Rhys himself still lived, and for many years after, but his hair had turned completely grey. In the morning, John Jones was found dead in his bed.

And so the story ended – but there was a twist in the tale. Upon further questioning, an ulterior motive for the mother's disproval of the union was brought to light:

> The informant stated that Mrs Jones in her younger days had been jilted by the elder Rhys, hence her antipathy to the marriage. It was not supposed that her posthumous appearances were intended to result so tragically as they actually did, but were made merely as a kind of protest against the marriage; from which we may deduce the moral that ghosts, no more than frail human-ity, can foresee the effects of terror on ignorant minds, and that they ought to be particularly careful how they 'turn up' at inconvenient hours to affright pale mortals; with which caution to ghosts in general, and those of mothers-in-law in particular, I close.

8

PARANORMAL HOAXES

Truly the nineteenth century is a most unfortunate period in the world's history for ghosts, and my readers will, I think, agree with me that fools – awful fools – are far more numerous than ghosts.

Not all of the ghost sightings reported in the Victorian press were considered to be genuine accounts of unexplained paranormal activity – far from it, in fact.

Ghosts of flesh and blood were just as popular, and there were many reports of how criminals, pranksters, the young and the easily led turned to the supernatural as a cover for committing a crime, as an excuse for creating mischief, or in some cases as an innocent mistake. These incidents were often readily explained, and could result in the perpetrators paying for their misconduct in court, where they faced ridicule along with their punishment.

We might laugh at them now, but some of the cases which follow could quite easily form the plot of an episode of a Scooby-Doo cartoon. In fact, in this first account from North Wales in 1887, a 'ghost' really was apprehended by a ghost-hunting dog:

> The inhabitants of the village of Rossett, near Chester, have been greatly alarmed by a 'ghost' that has been seen there recently. While a bicyclist was returning home the other night, the 'ghost' suddenly appeared before him. He fired a pistol at it, but failed to bring it down. Next night the 'ghost' approached a man who had a dog with him. The dog seized the 'ghost,' whereupon there were loud cries for assistance. The 'ghost' proved to be a villager not over fond of work, decked out in white clothes. The country-side has been kept in a state of terror by this man's masqueradings.

In this chapter, we will take a look at the creative – and not so creative – ways in which people tried to use the fear of the unknown to their own ends.

The Welsh Spring-heeled Jack

In Victorian England, the mysterious rogue known as Spring-heeled Jack caught the imagination of the public with his daring deeds and terrifying appearance. He inspired writers of fiction to expand upon his mythology, while inspiring others to imitate his actions by springing in his footsteps.

Spring-heeled Jack was first said to have been sighted in 1837, the year in which Queen Victoria acceded to the throne. Reports on his motives and distinctive clothing varied wildly, but he was considered by many to be supernatural, more devil than man, and his most popular trait was the ability to hurdle very high obstacles.

Spring-heeled Jack as depicted by an anonymous artist in a penny dreadful publication *c.* 1860. An image from *Humorous Poems …With a preface by A. Ainger, and … illustrations by C.E. Brock. L.P* by Thomas Hood (1893).

But these sightings were not restricted to England. Spring-heeled Jack was alive and well in Wales, where some considered him to be more of a Robin Hood-like character than a villain. Several copy-cat – or possibly genuine – sightings were attributed to the mysterious character, and any perpetrator who could leap a great distance was almost automatically assumed to be the man himself, such as in the following report from Swansea on New Year's Eve in 1896:

For some few years past the residents of the Mumbles and neighbourhood have each successive winter been disturbed during the night hours by the antics of individuals posing as a ghost, Spring-heeled Jack, and similar mysterious beings, and the custom has been kept up once more this winter, and remarkable stories have told of a person jumping over hedges, and performing such feats, when people have been going on their way home at midnight.

A gentleman living at the Mumbles and engaged in business at the Swansea Docks, relates that whilst proceeding home a man jumped out of the hedge and proceeded to perform the usual antics peculiar to the Mumbles ghost. The gentleman sprang upon the mysterious being, and after a bit of a struggle took the man near to a lamp, when to his surprise he identified the ghost as a young gentleman residing in Sketty. When asked the meaning of his strange antics, he said, 'It was only a joke.' The ghost is unlikely to disturb the peaceful minds of the inhabitants of the Mumbles any more this season.

In another account from Aberystwyth it was far from 'only a joke', where the local Spring-heeled Jack was said to have become violent:

The mysterious visitant haunts a lonely road just outside the town, and indulges, according to the local papers, in extraordinary acrobatic feats, frightens women and children, leaps walls twelve feet in height, and vanishes into space. On Sunday a resident came running into the town bearing marks of violent ill-treatment, to which he had, he declared, been subjected by some invisible influence; and to such a pitch has the panic grown that the haunted road is now patrolled by the members of the military drill class.

Strange lights at Wrexham Cemetery

Cemeteries were, for obvious reasons, popular locations for ghosts to make an appearance.

They were also popular locations for pranksters to cause a bit of mischief, and there are several reports from Wales during the Victorian era of troublemakers scaring their fellow townsfolk with strange sounds, sights and lights emanating from the local graveyard.

One incident, which took place in Wrexham Borough Cemetery in 1887, had everyone talking. But the joke backfired on the perpetrators, and saw one of the gang wind up in court as a consequence of imitating the spirit world.

It all began on a Wednesday night, when a vision in the cemetery 'attracted the attention of a number of people'. The news spread, and by the following night a large crowd had gathered outside the graveyard at 9 p.m., with the police called in to keep the peace:

> Sergeant Wynne and PC Rowland were soon on the spot and endeavoured to disperse the crowd, and also assisted the custodian to discover, if possible, the cause of the excitement. The ghostly character of the entertainment was produced, it appears, by the lighting of matches, and thereby bringing some of the statues and monuments into prominent relief. This amusement could only be carried on by human agency, and as no one was allowed to be on the premises after dark – the gates being locked at half-past five, the natural conclusion of the nervous and superstitious was that the agency was supernatural, and therefore a ghost. There appears to have been several operators on Thursday night, some of whom were recognised and will be summoned, while one was pounced upon in the act of striking a match, and while being collared by Mr Morris, the custodian, kicked him violently. The police present, however, were called and soon took him into custody, when he was locked up for the night, and brought before Messrs TC and G Bradley on Friday morning, when the facts of the case were deposed to by Mr Morris the custodian, PC Rowland, and a young man named Richard McDermot, and the prisoner, whose name is Mathias Davies, was fined 10s 6d and costs, or fourteen days in default. Other summonses are to be issued, and we opine that the ghost will be effectually laid.

Criminal damage

Cemeteries weren't the only spooky places to attract large gatherings. Reports of haunted houses also drew crowds in their hundreds, but while the troublemakers might have been inside the graveyards, when it came to homes, they were often found on the outside.

Large groups of restless onlookers, weary of waiting for some supernatural excitement to occur, could take matters into their own hands and create some fun of their own. One case from a house in Newport's

Mountjoy Street in 1894 saw boys from the neighbourhood 'gather round in groups at night time, in the vain hope of catching a glimpse of the spectral visitor'. When the spectre failed to make an appearance, they 'whiled away the time with throwing stones at the windows, until all the latter have been broken'.

They were caught by two plain-clothed policemen who had been called to the property by the homeowners, and one of the culprits, Charles Edwards, appeared at the borough police court to answer a charge of throwing a stone. He argued that the stone was in fact a marble, to which the unimpressed magistrates' clerk asked 'What? You don't expect to hit a ghost with a marble?' He was dismissed with a caution as the prosecutor chose not to proceed further.

In another case from Aberdare, a police court account records how another group – John Williams, Edward Morgan and John Evans – went one step further by breaking and entering into the property, and were 'charged with being drunk and riotous and making a disturbance':

Mr Phillips prosecuted on behalf of Mr James Hill. He stated that of late people have had an idea that one of the houses recently erected by Mr Hill, in Gadlys Road, was haunted, and this occasioned much excitement in the neighbourhood. On Saturday night last between 400 and 500 people assembled near the spot for the purpose of 'catching the ghost.' The defendants were amongst the number and were very drunk. John Williams said he had the power to send away the evil spirit, and that he had done so before. PC Gamblyn arrested Williams whilst kicking at the front door. The others were arrested by PC Porchase, who had secreted himself in the house. The men were roaring about the house and said they were 'looking for the ghost.' They were all taken to the station. They were fined 5s and costs each.

The servant's payback

Bogus reports of ghosts in houses also proved to be a handy way of getting revenge.

They appeared to be a particular favourite of servants, who would probably have a greater awareness of the properties than their owners, and could concoct all manner of strange events. Some of these were intended as harmless pranks – banging the pipes at night might send a shiver down the master's spine – but if they had an axe to grind with their employers, they could also turn malicious.

This was the case at The White Horse public house in Haverfordwest in 1851, when 'an instance of the gross superstition still prevalent in Wales' was revealed at the police court. But to the modern reader, what is possibly more remarkable than the event itself are some of the solutions which the locals suggested in order to rid themselves of the problem:

> The public house in Shut Street had, for some time, been the scene of nocturnal noises of a very mysterious nature, and stones and other missiles were occasionally showered in through the windows, no one could explain by what agency. Constables were set to watch the premises, but they failed to detect the cause of these annoyances. The consequence was that some of the neighbours pronounced the premises 'haunted,' and seriously meditated leaving the locality; while others ascribed the cause to the knowledge of the 'dark art' possessed by a simple domestic servant in the employ of the landlord. The landlord did not lack advisers at this critical period, some counselling that a clergyman should be called in to lay the 'haunting spirit,' others that blood should be drawn from the poor girl, as an effectual means of removing the 'spell,' while a third party, from fear of passing under the ban of the enchantress, suggested that the landlord should part with her on her pronouncing her benediction on himself and his family.
>
> While the credulous landlord was cogitating all the merits of the respective propositions, the spell was broken by the arrest of the servant girl in question, who had been observed by a policeman placed in ambush for the purpose, to creep stealthily into the yard and hurl a stone through the window. The supposed 'sorceress' was, therefore, taken before the magistrates, when she explained that she had been bribed to play off the tricks which had caused such consternation in the neighbourhood. She was severely admonished.

Unmasked by the vicar

In 1887, a 'ghostly visitant' in Swansea was 'successfully laid' by the local vicar.

The 'Caswell Ghost', as it became known, had been spotted numerous times in Caswell Bay and the road leading to the beach by an engineer of the Waterworks Company working at nearby Oystermouth. His job involved visiting the pumping engine house at all hours of the night, and he spoke of having seen a 'figure dressed in white, gliding along the road or flitting over the sands, and suddenly disappearing into the rocks which line the golden shores of that beautiful Bay'. He also:

> vowed vengeance on the ghost if he ever came within striking distance of it, for the many shocks he has had by its sudden appearance and disappearance on his lonely rounds of duty. For although he was not afraid of the Devil, this unsightly visitant had more than once caused his heart to bound with a quickened throb, his knees to shake, and his hair to stand on end.

But he was not alone in seeing the 'Caswell Ghost', and in the following report, the culprit was finally apprehended by the nearby village of Newton when he made an appearance at 8.30 p.m. one Sunday night:

> A lonely widower sitting disconsolate in his inglenook heard a knock at his door, and before he could rise and open it, the door silently opened, and the firelight's fitful gleam fell upon a figure dressed in white, with black face and arms, and in a voice grave and deep enough to have issued from the tomb itself, asked if it could have lodgings for the night. The man stood appalled at the sight before him, his knees smote, his tongue clave to the roof of his mouth; in silent horror he gazed at the apparition, which quietly backed out of the doorway and fled.
>
> The click of the garden gate aroused the horrified man from his stupor of surprise; he started, rubbed his eyes, looked – it was gone. Like a flash, it came upon him that his strange and unearthly visitor must be the Caswell Ghost. In the twinkling of an eye, he was out, and across the road to a neighbour's house, where, in spasmodic jerks, he told what he had seen. Fortified and encouraged by a draught, hastily swallowed, of his neighbour's supper beer, they both went out armed with the first weapons they could lay hold of. Children screaming, the patter of feet, and cries of fright, led them on the track his ghostship had taken, and as they went they picked up another brave man, who followed on. Turning to the left, up the village of Newton, they overtook an old woman, and speaking to her said – 'Aunty Mary, is that you?' 'Yes,' was the reply. 'Did you see anything pass here?' 'Yes, I saw something queer.' 'Which way did it go?' 'Why, into Will Owen's house.'

The ghost, not knowing that it had been followed, had in the meantime gone to Farmer Owen's house, and, knocking the door, it was opened by a granddaughter who screamed and bolted. A grandson went to the door, and he also saw and fled in dismay. The old farmer himself then went to see the cause of all this, and the ghost asked for lodgings; the brave old man's oaken staff went up, and would have descended with a sounding whack on the head of the ghost, but discretion being the better part of valour, even in a ghost, it silently backed away down the court – as a front garden is locally called – and again fled, but alas! right into the group of men talking to Aunt Mary.

Here, panic-struck, apparently by the array of arms around it, it stood in silent perplexity, while the men were also speechless from sheer wonderment and awe. Aunt Mary, however, had her wits about her, and said, 'Catch hold of it, and see what it is.' This had the desired effect, and one of them cried, 'I'll tackle it,' and he went for it. With a sidelong jump the ghost shied off and again fled, and rushing down the road plumped into a lot of people, mostly ladies, coming from Church service. Here was confusion worse confounded. Cries, screams, hysterical solos, told the effect the apparition had on the weak nerves of these ladies, startled out of their wits; some fainted, while others stood rooted to the spot spellbound with fright and terror; others ran screaming away, and soon a crowd was collected. Every house in Newton and Nottage poured out its wondering inhabitants.

The Vicar, walking quietly up the hill, heard all this, and looking up in the gloaming, he, too, saw the flying white figure, and gave chase, his coat flapping like wings, and seeing the men running, he called out to them, 'Catch him, catch him,' but the Vicar's university training gave him the advantage, and overtaking the ghost first, grasped it like a vice, and shaking it heartily cried, 'Speak, who are you?' (Ghost tries to wriggle out of his clutch). 'Here, Smith, just strip his hood off, and let us see who it is.' His bonnet, a long one, projecting well over his face, is readily grasped and torn away, and all looking cry: 'Oh, my prophetic soul! *Will Warlow.*'

The scene which followed is beyond description; and many were ready and willing to take summary vengeance on the practical joker, and but for the restraining hand and words of the Vicar, would have done so. The culprit tried hard to explain why and wherefore he had done so, saying it was to 'amuse his children,' that he had donned the dress. We are sorry that an otherwise steady and industrious man, civil and respectful in every way, should have so far forgotten himself and his neighbours as to have performed this silly trick.

In another report of the same case published in a different newspaper, the 'restraining hand and words' of the vicar did not hold back the crowd, and the 'Caswell Ghost' was given a 'good thrashing' for his efforts.

A case of mistaken identity

While there are some who might consider giving a 'good thrashing' to a practical joker fair punishment for pretending to be a ghost, there were also cases where the wrong person was assaulted.

In the next report from the *Barry Dock News* in 1892, a case of mistaken identity sees an innocent woman brutally beaten by a gang of vigilantes, who claimed to be patrolling the area after reading a report of a ghost in the same paper a fortnight before.

The perpetrators were James Moist and husband and wife Alfred and Rosina Palmer from Cadoxton, who were charged with assaulting Mary Ann Carroll of nearby Pencoedtre shortly after midnight. The following account of the events was recorded at the court hearing:

> Mrs Carroll left home in order to go to meet a woman who managed a shop for her at Holton Road. While going along the road towards Cadoxton, she met a crowd of about nine men and boys. There was also a woman amongst them. Alfred Palmer came up to her and held up his hands and said 'Stand back, you ghost!' He and his wife then struck her, after which Moist beat her badly, and 'blinded and choked her with blood.' He also threatened to blow her brains out. She was also thrown to the ground and again abused. She got up after a time, and went to the police station at Cadoxton in order to give information to the police. Several of the mob followed her to the station, especially the ringleaders (the defendants). The police were not at home, but Alfred Palmer called out to Mrs Davies (who opened her bedroom window) 'We have brought the Pencoedtre ghost, and we will have a drink with the reward'.

Evidence was given, and Timothy Mahoney, who had been a part of the gang which attacked Mrs Carroll, attempted to defend the trio by explaining that:

> having seen in the *Barry Dock News* that there was a ghost at Pencoedtre, about nine or ten persons went to watch the place which it was said was

haunted, and about half-past twelve they saw Mary Ann Carroll come across a field and get over the hedge on to the road. Alfred Palmer went on to meet her, and held up his hands, and said 'Stop ghost, stop!' She then called Mrs Palmer a b— whore, and told her to go home. Mrs Palmer then smacked Mrs Carroll in the face, when the latter picked up stones and threw them at the crowd. Moist consequently struck Mrs Carroll one blow in the face, but there were no further blows given.

The Bench, who refused to grant an adjournment, summed things up by saying that:

the woman had a perfect right to be out on the public road at night as well as the defendants. She evidently had been badly assaulted, and the magistrates were inclined to send the defendants to prison without the option of a fine. Taking all the circumstances into consideration, however, the defendants would be fined 40s each and costs, in default fourteen days' imprisonment each with hard labour.

A somnambulist at large

While there were those who would use the belief in ghosts to serve their own ends, not every artificially created eerie white form seen at night was a genuine attempt to scare or deceive, such as this case of a 'highly respectable young woman' from Treforest in 1892.

It all began at two o'clock one morning when:

a figure clad in white was seen coming down the Cardiff and Merthyr road from the direction of Pontypridd towards Glyntaff, Treforest. A hazy mist floating in the dim moonlight had the effect of magnifying the shrouded white figure. The road travelled by the white lady passes along the south-western outskirt of the common, which anciently bore the name Brydwen Ardd (Britannia's Garden).

It was at this spot that a contractor named Mr Jenkins, who worked for the Local Board, was 'ripping up the highway to lay down pipes for sewerage purposes', and it is his account which was related to the correspondent:

At night the open drains are guarded by watchmen, who have red lamps at regular intervals, as danger signals. At this particular spot the watchman is a veteran, who in his time has beheld many a corpse candle gliding through the gloom and it is nothing new for him to find his hair standing on end. The night, or, rather morning, was very still. No sound except that of the flowing Taff River broke on the ears of the faithful watchman. A sudden sound attracted his attention, and the same moment he beheld what seemed to him a large white figure standing in a tragic attitude in front of the residence of Mr RT Richards, local agent for Lady Llanover, and the watchman could not definitely decide what aspect the white figure had assumed, except that it seemed to be one of wild revenge!

But after a few seconds the figure started down the road, and, with a side glance and a motion with the palm of her hand directed towards the building as she took her departure, she made towards the red lamps and the watchman mustering something. The watchman felt inclined to bolt, but, hills being on one side and the canal on the other, he was hemmed in, and he trembled, and cried, 'O-O-O-Lor'!' The apparition came nearer with majesty in its step and defiance on its brow. It stopped opposite the watchman, who then saw that it wore something like a night-dress, and had a stocking placed like a coronet around the brow. One foot was naked and the other had a stocking on. The figure was that of a fine young woman.

She gazed intently upon the poor watchman, who leaned against the wall like one petrified. He did not, in the orthodox fashion, when addressing the ghost, cry with bated breath, 'Angels and ministers of grace defend us,' but a thundering 'Hoi.' The figure gave a jump like a skipping goat, and, gathering her skirts, such as they were, bolted down the highway, splashing the mud in all directions. She passed the Vicarage, and then up the Glyntaff Road, past 'Morien's' residence, and higher up the hill she reached her parent's house, and began to call, 'Mamma! Mamma! My hands are tied.' The door was quickly opened and she went inside, and it was not till then she became fully awake. She retired to rest at the usual time suffering from toothache. She has an indistinct recollection of hearing the sound of water falling, seeing dim moonlight, and walking through mud. But her recollections are like those of the incidents of a dream.

9

WEIRD WITTICISMS

Before concluding a book about ghosts in the Victorian press, it's worth taking a quick look at the effect they had on the wider culture as a whole.

As well as the news reports collected in this book, ghosts were also an increasingly popular genre of fiction, and stories from noted authors of the period such as Mary Elizabeth Braddon and Wilkie Collins were reprinted in the Welsh newspapers.

They were the subject of lengthy debates in the letters columns, and materialised in the most unlikely of places. In the following example, a ghost even made their way into a property sales advert:

SALE OF BRYN BRAS CASTLE, LLANRUG.– This castle and estate of about 80 acres has been sold by private treaty by Messrs Hedger and Mixer, of Whitehall, S.W. The castle is said to have cost some £20,000 to build, and has the reputation of being haunted, 'the ghost' being included in the sale.

Scarily bad puns

One common place for the supernatural to appear was in the regular joke columns of the press, although it should be stressed that the word 'joke' is used very loosely there – if these examples are anything to go by, Victorian humour has not aged well.

Presented below are a collection of jokes to feature the paranormal, but be warned – the punchlines are more terrifying than any of the ghastly tales contained in this volume.

At a spiritual séance a woman desired to communicate with her dead husband.

'Is it such a dreadful place, John?'

'Not at all; heaven is a delightful place.'

'Mr Medium,' said the widow, turning to that personage, 'you have called up the wrong party.'

★

At twelve o'clock sharp the sombre curtain moved, and the ghost entered the haunted chamber, gibbering gaily. 'But,' I protested, with vehemence, 'I am not in the least degree superstitious.' Whereupon the ghost uttered a howl of baffled rage and vanished. This experience of mine effectually silences all such as maintain that ghosts have no regard for convention.

★

Question: What course is it judicious to take at a spiritualistic séance?
Answer: Try to hit the happy medium.

★

First commercial traveller: The boot-black told me this morning that the room you slept in last night has the reputation of being haunted.
Second commercial traveller: Well, I shouldn't be surprised if that were so. I killed a few there last night myself.

★

'I don't know why you should say that empty old house is haunted.'

'Why, don't you see those ancient window curtains?'

'Yes, but …'

'Well, aren't they the shades of the departed?'

*

'Mister,' said the guest, nervously, 'I want to ask you a question. Isn't it a fact that my room is haunted?'

'It is,' said the clerk, 'but I didn't suppose you would mind it. The old man is perfectly harmless.'

'The old man?'

'Yes. The ghost you heard is the old fellow who built up the business. He can't rest easy because it goes on just as well as ever it did, now that he is gone.'

*

Fair homeseeker: I like the appearance of that house; but I wouldn't live in it for the world. People say it's haunted, and I am dreadfully nervous.

Agent (craftily): Yes, ma'am, they say that ghosts come out of every one of the thirty-two closets.

Fair homeseeker (setting her teeth hard): I'll take it!

*

Sir, the visitor in number 35 complains that the room is haunted.

Landlord: Indeed? Then put down on his bill, 'One ghost, 10 marks.'

*

'John, we must rent another house.'

'Why?'

'Every night I can hear ghostly sighing and whistling. It seems to come from the pipes, and I believe the place is haunted.'

'Shouldn't wonder. The former owner dropped dead with the plumber's bill in his hand.'

*

No wonder churchyards are haunted. After he has been kicked and cuffed all his life a fellow's ghost can't have a spark of vanity if it doesn't enjoy a quiet sit down in the moonlight to read the epitaph.

*

'No,' said the little widow emphatically. 'I will never attend another séance.'

'Why not?' asked her friend. 'Didn't you have any acquaintances among the spooks?'

'I am in doubt about the materializations.'

'Not distinct enough?'

'Well, it was this way: The medium said my husband was there and wanted to speak to me. It was too dark to see him plainly, but I thought I recognised the outlines of Jim, and I kissed him.'

'And was it Jim?'

'That's what I would like to know.'

'What makes you doubt it?'

'The spook had a lovely moustache.'

'Oh!'

'Jim never had one.' And the little widow looked thoughtful.

*

First friend: Do you believe in ghosts?
Second friend: Well, for years I have been living in a haunted house.
First friend: You don't say so! By whom is it haunted?
Second friend: By my tailor.

*

Do you believe there's such a thing as a haunted house?
Weeks: Oh, yes, indeed; but it depends a good deal upon how good-looking the girl is who lives in it.

*

Short: Do you know I've a strong suspicion that the house I'm living in is haunted?
Nabour: I know it is; I see the landlord's agent there nearly every day.

★

Wife (time, midnight): Hark, dear. I hear the rustling of silk and the clank of chains.
Husband: You do? Horrors! Then the reports are true. I was told the house was haunted.
Wife (much relieved): Oh, is that all? I was afraid Fido had broken loose and was tearing my new ball dress.

The Holy Ghosts

And finally, when it came to humour and the paranormal, the church was also a popular choice of subject, as these examples illustrate.

They have a haunted collecting box at a Methodist chapel in Bridgend. It has a handle at each end, and the other night a handle broke and the coppers went all over the floor. The curious thing is at the next meeting precisely the same thing happened, and the Church is now trying to find out who is the Jonah who puts in impious pennies.

★

In olden times the clergy were supposed to possess supernatural powers, in addition to their ordinary gifts. The Rev. Mr Huntington, of Tenby, tells us that a deputation once came to his predecessor, Dr Humphreys, requesting him to lay a ghost which haunted their parish. On his asking why they came to him when they had a parson of their own, they explained that it was only an Oxford scholar who could lay a ghost. 'I am afraid, then,' said the doctor, anxious to be let off without giving offence, 'you have come to the wrong man, for you can see I am a Cambridge man.'

★

An amusing tale is going the rounds concerning an old Welsh preacher who was travelling about South Wales collecting for his chapel. He was preaching one night – with, of course, a collection in view – at a country chapel. A certain nobleman, with a Welsh title, was on his way home from shooting. A shower of rain came on, and the nobleman and his friends turned into the porch to shelter. The sermon was in English, and the noble lord was so struck by what he heard that at the close of the service – which took place almost immediately – he went up to the preacher, and told him how much he admired him. Said he 'I would invite you to the castle, but we are full, with the exception of a haunted room.' 'I don't mind that at all,' said the blunt old preacher; and so he went to the castle for the night. The company were mightily excited over the idea of his sleeping in this room, and asked him next morning at breakfast what had happened. 'Oh,' said he, 'The ghost came in at twelve o'clock.' A shudder ran round the table. 'Yes' – said they, bending forward eagerly. 'Oh,' said the old man, 'I presented him my collecting book, and he immediately vanished.' It turned out that it was the ghost of a miser.

BIBLIOGRAPHY

Archive resources

The National Library of Wales, Aberystwyth
www.newspapers.library.wales
West Glamorgan Archive Service, Swansea
www.swansea.gov.uk/westglamorganarchives

Further reading

Blum, Deborah, *Ghost Hunters* (Arrow, 2007)
Clarke, Roger, *A Natural History of Ghosts: 500 Years of Hunting for Proof* (Penguin, 2003)
Pearsall, Ronald, *Table-Rappers: The Victorians and the Occult* (The History Press, 2004)
Weisberg, Barbara, *Talking to the Dead: Kate and Maggie Fox and the Rise of Spiritualism* (Bravo, 2004)

REFERENCES

1 Wild Wales

Epigraph: *South Wales Echo* 8 January 1897
The two-headed phantom
Usk Observer 1 November 1856
A wild night by the romantic lakes
North Wales Chronicle and Advertiser for the Principality 26 December 1885
The haunted hiding place
North Wales Express 8 September 1893
The Weekly News and Visitors' Chronicle 27 August 1897
The murdered knight
Weekly Mail 3 July 1897
A phantom coach with a headless driver
Flintshire Observer 12 December 1895

2 Haunted Homes

Epigraph: *Evening Express* 8 September 1899
South Wales Echo 16 January 1897
Flintshire Observer 12 December 1895
Wraith of a murderer stalks abroad
South Wales Daily Post 13 October 1899
Lively doings at Burry Port
South Wales Daily Post 23 March 1899
South Wales Daily News 30 March 1899
South Wales Daily News 29 March 1899
Whisked away by a hideous apparition

South Wales Echo 28 October 1893
South Wales Daily News 31 October 1893
Cardiff Times 11 November 1893
Cardiff's Lady in Grey
Evening Express 11 October 1893
A rival to Hamlet's father
South Wales Daily Post 8 November 1895

3 Talking with the Dead

Epigraph: *South Wales Daily News* 16 December 1891
Barry Herald 10 November 1899
The Alfred Russel Wallace page: http://people.wku.edu/charles.smith/wallace/
    S478.htm
Evening Express 23 April 1894
Séances in Wales
South Wales Daily News 16 January 1878
The touch of deathlike fingers
The Cambrian 5 December 1879
Spirit faces by candlelight
The Cambrian 24 January 1873
The language of heaven
Evening Express 22 October 1895

4 The Victorian Ghost Hunters

Epigraph: *Rhyl Advertiser* 19 November 1887
Western Mail 7 June 1884
Evening Express 2 September 1895
A call for scientific investigation
Evening Express 1 August 1900
Off with her head
Weekly Mail 27 September 1884
The secrets of Castell Moel
The Welshman 27 September 1895
Terrors of the night
North Wales Express 14 January 1887
North Wales Express 21 January 1887

5 Poltergeist Activity

Epigraph: *Weekly Mail* 21 February 1885
North Wales Chronicle and Advertiser for the Principality 6 February 1858
Startling noises down on the farm

The Cambrian News 23 July 1880
Evening Express 7 July 1897
South Wales Echo 29 January 1889
Strange rappings and stranger fancies
Evening Express 8 September 1899
South Wales Daily Post 7 September 1894
The Woman in White
South Wales Echo 16 January 1897
South Wales Echo 18 January 1897
South Wales Echo 21 January 1897
Terrifying nocturnal visits
Weekly Mail 2 December 1882

6 The Ghosts of Industry

Epigraph: Sikes, Wirt *British Goblins; Welsh Folk-Lore, Fairy Mythology, Legends, and Traditions* (1880)
South Wales Daily Post 1 March 1894
The haunted ironworks
Western Mail 17 August 1881
Western Mail 20 August 1881
The Pit of Ghosts
South Wales Daily News 12 March 1890
Cardiff Times 15 March 1890
South Wales Echo 30 April 1890
The Cambrian 14 March 1890
The Fright of the Morfa Colliers
Evening Express 11 December 1895
Blood-curdling ghosts of the mines
Evening Express 16 December 1895
Western Mail 17 December 1895
A Christmastime caution
Wrexham Advertiser 28 December 1895
Flintshire Observer 9 January 1896
The ghost train from the future
Aberystwith Observer 19 November 1864

7 Sacred Ground and Superstition

Epigraph: *Carmarthen Journal* 4 October 1889
The mysterious white mist
Denbighshire Free Press 14 September 1901
The funeral procession of spirits

Pontypridd Chronicle 30 December 1898
Violent retribution
Llangollen Advertiser 18 April 1879
The mysteries of the corpse candles
Weekly Mail 21 March 1885
The Welsh Jack-o'-lantern
Pontypridd Chronicle 18 November 1898
Revenge from beyond the grave
North Wales Express 24 December 1886

8 Paranormal Hoaxes

Epigraph: *The Cambrian News* 7 November 1873
South Wales Echo 3 February 1887
The Welsh Spring-heeled Jack
South Wales Daily Post 1 January 1897
Evening Express 5 March 1901
Strange lights at Wrexham Cemetery
Wrexham Advertiser 22 October 1887
Criminal damage
South Wales Echo 23 April 1894
Aberdare Times 10 October 1874
The servant's payback
North Wales Chronicle and Advertiser for the Principality 26 April 1851
Unmasked by the vicar
The Cambrian 22 April 1887
A case of mistaken identity
Barry Dock News 1 January 1892
A somnambulist at large
Pontypridd Chronicle 25 November 1892

9 Weird Witticisms

Carnarvon and Denbigh Herald 8 October 1897
Scarily bad puns
Aberdare Times 15 August 1885
Cardiff Times 10 February 1900
South Wales Daily News 3 July 1896
Evening Express 2 December 1896
Evening Express 25 July 1900
Barry Herald 27 August 1897
Cardigan Observer 9 June 1894

South Wales Echo 4 February 1896
Carnarvon and Denbigh Herald 22 July 1892
South Wales Echo 22 February 1894
Cardiff Times 19 December 1896
Cardiff Times 28 January 1893
Cardiff Times 3 September 1892
Evening Express 11 November 1901
Aberdare Times 24 May 1890
The Holy Ghosts
South Wales Daily Post 12 April 1897
Evening Express 24 November 1892
Aberdare Times 17 August 1889

INDEX

DO YOU HAVE
A GHOST STORY?

This might be the end of this book of Welsh ghost stories, but I am always on the lookout for more spooky tales for upcoming projects.

If you've ever had any paranormal experiences of your own, from hearing strange noises in the middle of the night, to seeing a full-bodied apparition in a haunted house, then I'd love to hear from you.

These can be first-hand accounts of inexplicable phenomena, or tales which have been passed down through the generations from any time period. Maybe even just local gossip or hearsay that might provide an interesting lead.

If you have a story to share, get in touch with me here: Mark Rees; mark@reviewwales.co.uk

The History Press — The destination for history — www.thehistorypress.co.uk